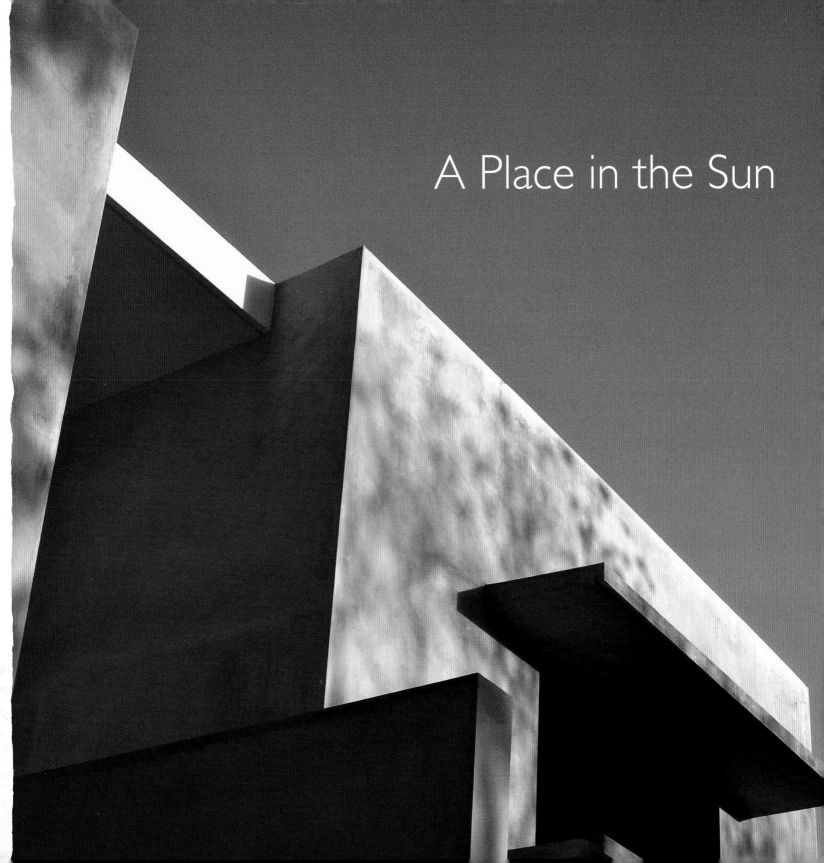

A Place in the Sun

A Place in the Sun

Green Living and the Solar Home

Stephen Snyder
Introduction by John Hix

First published in the United States of America in 2014 by
RIZZOLI INTERNATIONAL PUBLICATIONS, INC.
300 Park Avenue South, New York, NY 10010
www.rizzoliusa.com

ISBN-13: 978-0-8478-4229-2
Library of Congress Control Number: 2013948342

Distributed to the U.S. Trade by Random House, New York
Printed and bound in China
Designed by Abigail Sturges

2014 2015 2016 2017 2018 / 10 9 8 7 6 5 4 3 2 1

Page 1: John Hix Studios, Casa Solaris, Vieques, Puerto Rico

Pages 2–3: Robert M. Cain, Architect, Briar Creek Farm,
Varnville, South Carolina

Left: David Stark Wilson, WA Design, Stinson Beach House,
Marin County, California

Contents

6 Acknowledgments

8 Introduction *John Hix*

10 *Sunset* Magazine 2012 Idea House

14 Contemporary Timber Frame

20 Cherokee Mixed-Use Lofts

24 Step Up on Fifth

30 Briar Creek Farm

38 RainShine House

50 Brooks Avenue Residence

60 Juanita Verde

68 Esther's Island Retreat

74 Helenowski Residence

82 Hix Island House

92 Caribbean Villa

98 Ferrous House

106 OS House

114 Hacienda Ja Ja

120 Leon Springs Residence

126 Greenbridge

136 Make It Right Flow House

140 The Visionaire

150 Ocean Avenue Residences

156 Wine Creek Road Residence

164 Wilke-Duffy House

170 Zero Impact House

176 EnV

184 Seneca House

192 UCSD Rita Atkinson Residences

204 Berkeley Bungalow

212 Stinson Beach House

220 Resources

223 Recommended Reading

224 Photography Credits

Acknowledgments

Left: Lake|Flato Architects,
Hacienda Ja Ja,
Alamo Heights, Texas

Opposite: Lake|Flato
Architects, Leon Springs
Residence, Bexar County, Texas

This book would not exist without the immeasurable talent, generosity, and helpfulness of the following people. I am forever in their debt. Thanks, first of all, to John Hix for his incredible hard work, generosity, patience, and sage advice; David Morton, Douglas Curran, Abigail Sturges, and Andrea Monfried at Rizzoli; and my literary agent, Jeanne Fredericks. Photographers Antonio Cuellar, Doug Edmunds, Matt Dula, Great Island Photography, Paul Hultberg, Barbara Karant, Rob Karosis, David A. Lee, Nic Lehoux, John Edward Linden, John J. Macaulay, Charles Mayer, Frank Ooms, J. D. Peterson, Augusta Quirk, Peter Murdock, Robert Reck, Barry Rustin, Mark Singer, Romina Tonucci, and E. Spencer Toy all deserve special mention. I thank Dwight DeMay at Hart Howerton; David Stark Wilson AIA, Chris Parlette AIA, and Eoi Takagi at WA Design; Jacek Helenowski and Mariusz Bleszynski AIA, LEED AP; Lynne Berry at Siegel & Strain; Rosemary Wardell; Craig Copeland and Sharif Aggour at Pelli Clarke Pelli; Jeremy Bonin AIA, NCARB, LEED AP and Kimberly Bonin of Bonin Architects; Kira Gould of William McDonough + Partners; Bart Mitchell and Matthew Stannard at Stillwater Dwellings; Elizabeth Walden at Quinn & Co.; the Albanese Organization; Christopher Lucas and Paul McCreesh, the GreenGuys; Eric Corey Freed LEED AP; Donna Gorman and Roger Johansson; Robert M. Cain FAIA, LEED AP and Molly Lay; Ashley Andrews at Jennings; Ryan Cooper at the Marketing Directors; Debby and Jack; Dana Smith at Dadascope; Robert Hoang, Sierra Haight, and Denise De Leon at Lake|Flato Architects; Claudia Hura M.D. and David Stump M.D.; Emily Sano and Gilson Riecken; Emily Hodgdon at Brooks + Scarpa; Michelle M. Laboy and Maryann Thompson; Bob Duffy and Karen Wilke; Sebastian Schmaling; Joe Valerio FAIA, NCARB and Joe Lawton at Valerio Dewalt Train Associates; Taylor Royle at Make It Right; Isabelle Duvivier AIA, LEED AP; and Linda Jassim at Studio J Marketing. I am especially grateful to my family for all of their love, patience, and support.

Introduction

John Hix

Right: John Hix Studios,
Hix Island House,
Vieques, Puerto Rico

Study nature, love nature, stay close to nature. It will never fail you.
— *Frank Lloyd Wright*

I saw many huts that the natives made [in Africa.] There were no architects there. I came back with multiple impressions of how clever was the man who solved the problems of sun, rain and wind.
— *Louis Isadore Kahn*

Biologist D'Arcy Wentworth Thompson, in his seminal book *On Growth and Form*, explained that subtle environmental forces cause natural life forms (cells, plants, and animals) to evolve by natural selection, or survival of the fittest. Human habitats, buildings, and community designs should likewise be strongly influenced by these natural forces. If the form and skin of architecture take these forces into account, we can reduce our need for oil, coal, and atomic reaction. If we move away from hermetically sealed, energy-dependent buildings, we can decrease our electricity consumption. We should strive to get as close to zero energy use as possible.

In this book, Stephen Snyder has assembled a collection of contemporary architects who convert environmental technology, in varying degrees, into art by choosing ecologically sound materials and by recognizing a site's natural characteristics. Because regional topography, local vegetation, and appropriate construction methods are intrinsic parts of their aesthetic decisions, these architects help reverse the damage wrought by massive energy consumption. Instead of adhering to a prescriptive set of forms endorsed by fashionable trends or to the comfortable reassurances of an easily accessible design vocabulary, these buildings are based on the unique challenges of each site.

All architects should strive for a balance between the natural environment and the protective functions essential to buildings. This balance can best be achieved with climate-related design and a commitment to energy efficiency. Architects should learn from the vernacular buildings in the region around each site. Indigenous buildings, like living creatures, evolved through human selection of the most resilient, durable, and long-lasting dwellings. To broaden an understanding of the interface between raw nature and a controlled inhabited environment, architects can learn from similar climatic conditions that occur in different locations around the world.

I am attracted to the houses in this book that, through their configuration and, in some cases, their skin, modulate existing climatic conditions to provide protection and comfort for the occupants. It is in designing a building's skin that forces in the natural environment may be harnessed. The envelope can be made to admit solar heat, fresh air, cooling breezes, humidity, and natural light. Mechanical systems need be called on only when the internal environment cannot be tempered organically. I believe there is more potential in the study and development of a building's skin than in structural innovation.

We should learn that the house does not contain the machine: the house is the machine.

Sunset Magazine 2012 Idea House

Healdsburg, California
Architect: Blu Homes

Every year since 2005, *Sunset* magazine has sponsored an "idea house" to showcase trends in homebuilding and remodeling. In 2012, *Sunset* partnered with prefabricated house builder Blu Homes for the annual feature. Blu's iconic Sunset Breezehouse had debuted in *Sunset* magazine in 2005, and for the 2012 Idea House, Blu Homes developed a "next generation" Breezehouse on a breathtaking site in Sonoma County discovered by owners Jack and Rosemary Wardell.

Both the original Breezehouse and the updated, more spacious version, which is LEED certified, are based on the dogtrot homes of the southeastern United States. In these vernacular residences, built in the days before air conditioning, a well-ventilated central area between living spaces promoted ample airflow. In the Breeze-house, the living and dining areas, or Breeze-space, replicate the dogtrot with energy-efficient glass walls that can be opened to the outdoors at both front and back. The metal butterfly roof and clerestory windows invite sunlight into the Breezespace. During the day, the floors and walls absorb the sun's heat; at night, it is slowly released back into the home.

On either side of the Breezespace are modular wings that contain the kitchen, two bedrooms, four bathrooms, a separate den and office (which can be used as additional bedrooms), a wine cellar, and laundry and mechanical rooms. Wide hallways promote the flow of air throughout the residence. A detached Breezepod serves as a guest cottage. The indoor-outdoor interplay of the Breezehouse is underscored by numerous outdoor living spaces and an exterior

water feature, a two-by-eight-foot fountain with two spouts.

Manufactured in Blu's Vallejo, California, factory, the residence was "unfolded" at the site in Healdsburg in a matter of weeks, not months or years. The team included Blu Homes architect Joseph Remick, interior designer Sharon Portnoy, landscape architect Steve Hinderberger, and landscape designers and stylists Bonnie Gemmell and Jessy Berg from Habitat Design.

Research into materials and methods— cutting-edge computer modeling, innovative use of steel, and pioneering folding technology—makes Blu's homes easier to erect and less costly than site-built homes, even than many other prefabs. A bright, open design makes for living spaces that feel deceptively large; in reality, the relatively small footprint generates a smaller carbon footprint.

Blu Homes made the new Breezehouse even greener than the original by adding a solar thermal water heater, which heats the house via a Warmboard radiant floor system and provides hot water for domestic use. Among the host of additional green features are low-VOC paints from Benjamin Moore's Aura product line; maintenance-free fiber-cement siding products; structural insulated panels, which provide a tight air seal that contributes greatly to the overall efficiency of the residence; and a high R-value wall assembly with rain screen, exterior insulation, and blown-in wall cavity insulation. The structural steel and light steel in the home are up to 77 percent recycled. Manufacture of the steel frame produced less waste than lumber (2 percent versus 20 percent); the frame itself is recyclable. The Idea House also features bamboo floors throughout and low-flow water fixtures.

Prefab Homes

Architects and manufacturers have been developing prefabricated homes—kit, mobile, panelized, and modular homes—since the early twentieth century. In architecture, the term "prefab" generally describes a modular house that is manufactured off-site, in a climate-controlled factory, and then transported to the building site for assembly. Prefab homes offer many options for size, height, and layout. Prefab house construction is characterized by efficiency of scale and lack of waste, making it a popular choice for green homes.

Contemporary Timber Frame

Grafton County, New Hampshire
Architect: Bonin Architects & Associates

Grid-Tied Solar Electric Systems

Solar electric systems, also known as photovoltaics or PV, produce direct current electricity; an inverter converts the direct current to alternating current for home use. Grid-tied solar systems transmit their power to the electric utility grid. In most states, utilities offer credits to homeowners for power that is sent to the grid but not consumed. This credit can be used when the homeowner uses more power than is created. These agreements are called "net metering" or "net billing" and are a major benefit of installing solar power.

The clients for this timber-frame residence in the Dartmouth–Lake Sunapee region of New Hampshire had planned to build a new home for several years. They gathered a comprehensive file of magazine clippings—particularly from magazines focused on wood homes—and had settled on a timber frame, believing it would best suit both their lakefront property and the rustic, natural charm of the region. Other objectives included maximizing the lakefront views, accommodating extended family stays, entertaining friends, and living in an energy-efficient way, mostly on one floor.

At a local home show, the owners attended a lecture on green building by architect Jeremy Bonin, which reinforced their plan to build sustainably. Once they saw examples of his eco-friendly timber-frame work, they chose him to direct their project. Bonin worked with the constraints of the clients' property, carefully adjusting the design of the house for optimal views, solar exposure, and low-profile fit within the context. The residence has a surprisingly private feel despite its nearby neighbors.

The homeowners were fascinated with all of the details involved in a custom house project and wanted to be intimately involved with the building process. They planned a "hundred-year approach" to the residence. They aspired to a house that would last indefinitely, even against the background of an uncertain future; the systems they would install would allow future owners to meet the challenges of climate change and limited natural resources.

Geothermal heating and cooling conditions the interior spaces, with radiant heat on the lower concrete floor and forced hot air upstairs. Solar hot water is currently the most affordable and cost-effective renewable energy system; in the near future, the clients plan to add photovoltaic panels for solar electricity.

Local and sustainable materials have been specified wherever possible. The homeowners trekked to quarries in nearby Vermont in search of just the right stone. That close involvement has fostered an almost unprecedented appreciation for the effort involved in designing and building the house. The husband, a surgeon, was wowed by the intricate and meticulous stonework of the hearth. While the attention to detail had its challenges—colored gels from the theater department at nearby Dartmouth College were required to properly warm the LED lights used in the rafters—the rewards have proven to be proportional to the effort.

Wood inside and out brings warmth to the structure and softens its edges. Douglas fir keyed beams, bound with iron bands for strength and flexibility, are beautiful in form and especially in function, since they allow for a post-free open floor plan. The beams also provide framework for the structural insulated panels. SIPs consist of a core of rigid insulation with a layer of sheathing on one or both sides; they permit substantially less air infiltration and reduce thermal bridging between exterior and interior. SIPs offer higher performance than many conventional construction methods as well as high continuous R-values.

Cabinets and finish materials were sourced from New Hampshire and Vermont companies, and sealants, adhesives, and paints are all low- or no-VOC. Lighting is LED or next-generation-LED compatible, furthering the already low energy consumption of the home.

Style, function, and energy efficiency are united with durable materials, quality construction, and attention to detail in this forward-looking green home. Architect Bonin and the builder, Jay Tucker of Old Hampshire Designs, concurred with the motto the homeowners took for themselves: "Enjoy the process." Since then, the phrase has become the clients' advice to prospective green homeowners.

Cherokee Mixed-Use Lofts

Los Angeles, California

Architect: Brooks + Scarpa (formerly Pugh + Scarpa)

Cherokee Lofts is the most advanced and distinctive mixed-use housing project in Los Angeles. In fact, it was designed to be the "greenest" LEED Platinum development in the state of California. The building honors Cherokee Studios, a legendary recording studio, the MGM and Republic Studios before it, and all the artists who have recorded music on the site, from Frank Sinatra to David Bowie to Dave Matthews.

Cherokee Lofts consists of twelve market-rate lofts and 2,800 square feet of retail space. The five-story structure comprises one level of underground parking, parking and retail on the first floor, three floors of living spaces, and a rooftop deck and green roof. The building was inspired by a series of paintings by British artist

Patrick Hughes titled *Perspectivity*. These works appear to change and move. Architect Brooks + Scarpa interpreted this concept in an operable double-facade system. Occupants are able to adjust the screens, virtually redesigning the building front "live" from within the space. The perforated anodized-aluminum panels sparkle in the sun and glow at night; they provide shade, reduce noise, and enhance privacy while allowing for spectacular views, natural light, and ventilation from ocean breezes.

The planning and design emerged from an investigation of passive design strategies, notably locating and orienting the building to control solar cooling loads; shaping the building for exposure to prevailing winds; sculpting the building to induce buoyancy for natural

ventilation; designing windows to maximize daylighting and natural ventilation; shading south-facing windows and minimizing west-facing glazing; utilizing low-flow fixtures and stormwater management; and planning the interior to enhance daylight and natural airflow. These tactics alone make this building more than 40 percent more efficient than is required by California Title 24, the state's energy-efficiency program.

A thirty-kilowatt photovoltaic solar system pro-vides electricity for all common areas and more than 10 percent of the building's heating and hot water. Located within walking distance of many community services, Cherokee Lofts receives a high rating—Walker's Paradise—from Walk Score, an organization that promotes walkable neighbor-hoods. A green roof provides planted areas for the occupants; it also keeps the building better insulated, cleans the air, and reduces stormwater runoff. Dual-flush toilets, efficient plumbing fixtures, hot-water circulators, and drought-tolerant land-scaping limit water use. All stormwater runoff is collected in an underground retention basin located in the public right-of-way, the first such stormwater system in the city of Los Angeles.

An advanced variable-refrigerant-flow system cools and warms floors, ceilings, and walls to create a temperate environment suited to over-all health, comfort, and energy efficiency. Green materials and products, including those that are recycled, renewable, and contain low or no VOCs, are used throughout.

Solar Hot Water

Solar domestic hot water or solar thermal systems offer a way to use renewable energy in a home at a cost far lower than that of photovoltaics. SDHW is frequently used in radiant flooring for space heating. Solar-hot-water collectors are flat plates that look similar to PV panels or evacuated glass tubes; the collectors can be installed anywhere the sun will strike them for six to eight hours daily.

Step Up on Fifth

Santa Monica, California

Architect: Brooks + Scarpa

Passive and Active Solar Strategies

A passive solar home uses natural cooling and heating rather than fossil fuels or energy-consuming mechanical devices to condition a house. Passive solar heating systems capture solar energy within the building and slowly radiate that heat throughout the day. Active solar strategies include mechanical renewable energy systems such as photovoltaic systems, which use solar panels to produce electricity, and solar thermal systems, which use the sun's energy to provide radiant heating or domestic hot water.

Step Up on Fifth provides residences and services for the homeless and mentally disabled population of Santa Monica. Forty-six studio apartments support Step Up's goal of offering permanent affordable housing to those in recovery. A primary objective of the Brooks + Scarpa team was to improve the quality of living—and the quality of design—of conventional affordable-housing projects.

The main facade, which faces northwest, is a dramatic composition of water-jet-anodized aluminum panels; these also protect from the sun and create privacy for the residents. Asymmetrical horizontal openings on the south faces filter direct sunlight and foster a sense of security for the emotionally sensitive occupants while lending an unexpected visual depth to the structure. Community rooms are located on every other

floor of the building; these overlook private internal courtyards. These community rooms and courtyards are the principal social spaces for building residents.

Step Up passively adapts to the temperate arid climate of Southern California. Building components are sited to take advantage of abundant natural ventilation and light and to control heat gain and heat loss. The courtyards are arranged to induce airflow and provide maximum natural light. The rooms are kept cool by cross ventilation; double-glazed low-E windows (low-emittance coatings of microscopic metallic layers minimize heat transfer); and insulation that boosts thermal values 50 percent above conventional wood-frame construction (R21 in the walls and R30 in the roof).

The building is loaded with energy-saving and environmentally benign or sustainable devices. Construction waste was recycled; natural materials and materials with recycled content also maximize resource conservation. A stormwater catch-basin and filter system (hidden in the front planter) captures and treats all of the rainwater falling on the site. Each apartment is equipped with Energy Star refrigerators, water-saving low-flow toilets, and a high-efficiency hydronic (hot water) solar thermal system for heat. Compact fluorescent lighting is used throughout the facility, which exceeds state-mandated Title 24 energy measures by 26 percent.

Materials with recycled content include carpet (25 percent post-consumer content), gypsum board (3 percent pre-consumer and 5 percent post-consumer), concrete (at least 10 percent fly ash), and insulation (formaldehyde-free, at least 20 percent recycled glass cullet). Low-VOC paint is used inside the building, and the floors in common areas are sealed, exposed concrete slab or natural linoleum.

South Coast Air Quality Management District (the Los Angeles air-pollution-control agency) and Green Seal regulations determined indoor air quality. Finishes were minimized—the exterior stucco was integrally colored to avoid any need for exterior paint—or even eliminated. Off-gassing was likewise decreased. Ninety-eight percent of the volume is daylit; 96 percent can be ventilated with operable windows.

Step Up is located only six blocks from the beach, and retaining water on the site is a major ingredient in the city's effort to rehabilitate Santa Monica Bay. All precipitation and stormwater is collected in a subsurface infiltration system. Once it is cleaned of ollutants, the captured water is returned to the groundwater. Landscaping consists of native and drought-tolerant plants. A drip irrigation system may be adjusted seasonally, and a substantial amount of gravel allows water to percolate into the ground.

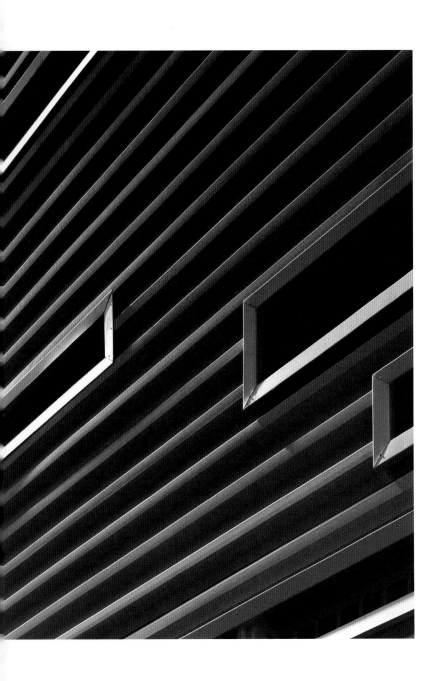

Briar Creek Farm

Varnville, South Carolina
Architect: Robert M. Cain, Architect

Briar Creek Farm is a new residence for a family of five. Architect Robert Cain, when he first walked the several-hundred-acre farmland site with the owner, was intrigued by several features in close proximity: an old borrow pit from the construction of the adjacent "hardtop" road; a high point occupied by maturing mixed hardwoods, many of them live oaks; a large north-south glade bounded by live oaks on the west and a double row of slash pines on the east; a generous corn field that saw many fall dove hunts; and acres of land newly planted with *Pinus palustris,* the slow-growing but magnificent longleaf pine.

Cain situated the house to take advantage of and blend into these features. By removing a small swath of young pines, he created an east-

west axis for the house that provides the ideal solar orientation; in addition, the cleared area opens views east to the field and west to the pit, which will one day become a lake. The house is split into three staggered shotguns to optimize views and ventilation; transparent "bridges" stitch the whole together. The intersection between the east-west axis and the north-south glade positions the central volume, which contains the great room. The entrance, master suite, and office are positioned at the northwest, and the children's and utility areas at the southeast.

The owners requested a house filled with light, views, and cross ventilation. The vernacular shotgun house "ain't nothing but a way to keep cool" during the hotter months, particularly on

the southern coastal plain. Windows on both sides take advantage of the slightest breeze, as do the linked shotguns. Also contributing to performance in this climate are the east-west orientation and extended eaves and gable ends, all of which minimize solar gain.

The trees to the north and west and the open areas to the south and east create a microclimate of which the owners took full advantage. The oaks shelter the home from direct afternoon sun; the house axis is tilted slightly to reduce the overall solar exposure. In the heat of the day, open areas superheat and create rising thermals that pull air from the cooler hardwood areas. Fresh breezes waft through the house. Also promoting natural cooling are the crawl space and utility basement area under the structures. Insulated and unvented, the base-

ment has a vapor barrier and accommodates all duct runs.

Reclaimed old-growth heart pine is used for trim, cabinetry, flooring, ceilings, and furniture. Beams and various details are composed of salvaged, locally manufactured steel. Sustainable materials include locally produced wood and masonry products, low-VOC paints and coatings, and recycled decking.

A high-efficiency open-loop water-source heat pump connected to shallow wells harnesses the high water table of the coastal plain, providing economical heating and cooling. Water from the system charges the lake after use. In addition, landscaping consisting of native drought-resistant species limits maintenance and irrigation needs.

Thermally Broken Glazing

Generally windows are a thermal weak point in the building envelope. Providing non-conductive materials between frames and air gaps between glass helps to minimize heat gain and loss. In home construction thermally broken glazing refers to windows in which air or gas between the panes inhibits the transfer of thermal energy through the glass.

RainShine House

Decatur, Georgia
Architect: Robert M. Cain, Architect

The RainShine House, a two-story, 2,800-square-foot structure on a third-acre lot, is named for its key design features. A butterfly roof captures rainfall, directing it to a rainwater harvesting system located in the basement (Rain); on this roof is a photovoltaic system that takes advantage of the southern exposure (Shine). RainShine was constructed under the LEED for Homes Program Pilot Rating System. The house exceeded the requirements by eleven points and is the first modernist residence in the southeastern United States to achieve LEED Platinum certification.

Designed as a retirement residence with ample provision for visitors, the RainShine House has common areas and the master bedroom on the first floor and guest bedrooms with an office loft on the partial second floor. The home features operable windows as well as large expanses of thermally broken glazing with solar shades to fulfill the owners' desire for as much natural ventilation as possible. Interior zones are defined by "thick walls" containing storage, bookshelves, pass-throughs, and building systems.

The butterfly roof is supported by steel beams spanned by exposed 1½-inch tongue-and-groove wood decking. The inverted form promotes rainwater collection and eliminates extensive gutter and downspout systems and the associated maintenance headaches. The roof floats above continuous clerestory windows.

Light shelves around the clerestory sills bounce natural light throughout the interior.

Located in the basement are five five-hundred-gallon RainHarvest cisterns that collect water for household use and landscape irrigation, a geothermal heat pump, desuperheaters, and an energy-recovery ventilator. Other sustainable components include water-based insulation materials, an LED lighting system, and the net-metered, roof-mounted, 3.1-kilowatt photo-voltaic system. The residence is so efficient that it is anticipated to consume only 43 percent of the energy expended by a similar home built to the standards of the International Energy Conservation Code.

The green aspects of this home extend to the landscaped site, which was designed by Lynn Saussy. All new plantings are native shrubs and grasses. Deciduous trees and shrubs shade the house in summer and allow sun to penetrate in winter. A grand deodar cedar protects the residence from the western sun, and two native parsley hawthorns will screen the southern sun but not the solar panels on the roof.

One of the most important LEED credits given to this house was for "extraordinary performance" in the selection of homeowner- and

Open-Cell Foam Insulation

Open-cell foam insulation, though not as structurally strong as closed-cell insulation, provides excellent air barrier properties, allows structural timbers to breathe, is more effective as a sound barrier than closed-cell, and is less expensive.

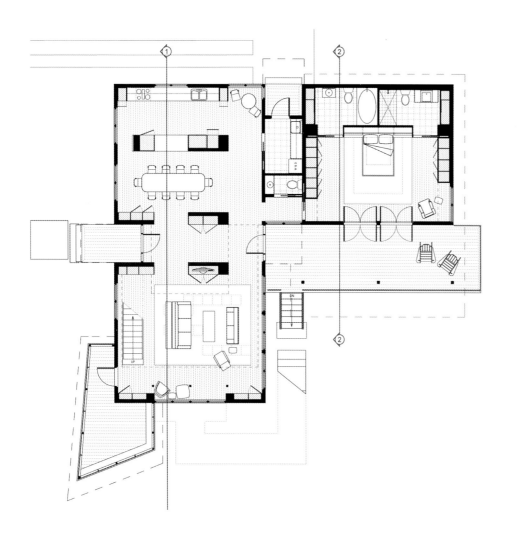

environment-friendly materials. All of the interior paints, stains, floor finishes, adhesives, and sealants are low- or no-VOC; the custom millwork is constructed of no-formaldehyde, 100-percent-recycled-content MDF; the solar shades are no-VOC; the concrete/glass countertops include 70 percent recycled content and the carpet tiles 40 percent; the wall insulation is formaldehyde-free; appliances and fixtures are highly efficient and conserve water. Exterior paints are low-VOC, as is the siding; the foundation waterproofing is a MERIT-certified (Materials with Environmentally Reduced Impact) green system. Even the products used to clean the house after construction were Green Seal certified. The residence is almost fully nontoxic.

The local concrete for the foundation contains 30 percent fly ash, and the heart-pine flooring was reclaimed from pre–Civil War police stables in Atlanta. The massive exterior doors were built from locally salvaged heart pine. The exterior decking is manufactured from postconsumer recycled plastic and waste wood. Many construction materials were sourced locally, minimizing heavy-truck transport to the site, and construction waste was recycled to reduce landfill impact. The coffee table and console in the living room were designed by the architect and built from old-growth longleaf pine salvaged from the police stables with a no-VOC, clear, water-based finish.

Brooks Avenue Residence

Venice, California

Architect: Isabelle Duvivier, Duvivier Architects

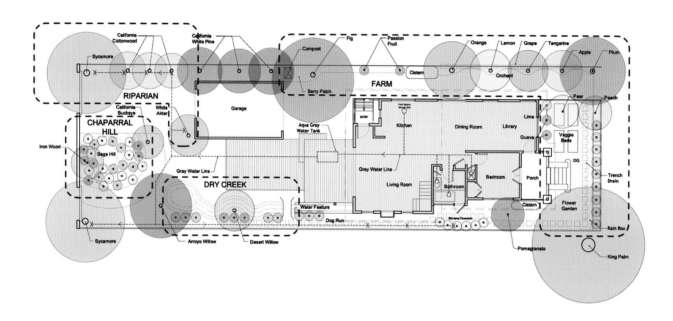

In 2009, architect and environmentalist Isabelle Duvivier purchased a dilapidated hundred-year-old home in a modest neighborhood on Brooks Avenue in Venice, California. She wanted to keep the feel of the Craftsman house, to blend into the neighborhood, but she had a second, larger goal—to reduce the environmental impact and energy footprint of the house through intelligent, experimental technologies in water, energy, and materials while also using natural light and floor-to-ceiling windows and doors to engage the natural environment. Without the requirement to meet a client's needs, the house became a personal learning laboratory for Duvivier.

Duvivier planned her renovation and addition to the Craftsman bungalow, now 1,700 square feet, in the context of the neighborhood as a

whole. She is designing a sustainable plan for the area, reimagining the streets and alleyways as part of a broader network of green infrastructure; permeable paving, street trees, and play areas are essential elements of the concept. The sailing form of the new second story blends with the existing house and respects the architectural history and scale of this beach neighborhood.

The U.S. Green Building Council awarded the Brooks Avenue Residence its 2012 Outstanding Home Award, which recognizes innovative multi- and single-family projects; in addition, it has been certified as LEED Platinum, which is unusual for a renovation. The house received 109 points, ranking it among the top ten LEED-rated homes in California and the top twenty-five LEED-rated homes nationally. Manifold

sustainable strategies and components were incorporated: daylighting schemes, ventilation (there is no need for air conditioning), and low-flow fixtures. Carefully placed windows, solar tubes, and skylights improve energy performance. All new walls are framed with 2x6s, and the insulation was installed as per Quality Insulation Installation guidelines. A four-kilowatt solar array produces a power surplus ten months out of twelve. High-efficiency appliances and Energy Star lighting (95 percent LED lights) result in a home that is 53 percent more efficient than dictated by California's Title 24 building-energy-efficiency standards.

Material was used in an ultra-efficient manner. Stair treads, doorjambs, and bookshelves are made from laminated hundred-year-old 2x4s that were reclaimed from the few walls removed from the bungalow. The existing Douglas fir floors were restored. The old cellulose insulation was composted on site; all excavated soil remains on the property (hence the sculptural "hills" in the backyard). The exterior siding, bathroom tiles, concrete countertops, insulation, and foundation are all high-recycled-content products. Seventy-six percent of construction waste was diverted from landfills.

A succinct, efficient water distribution system inside and outside the home was developed, according to low-impact principles, by the

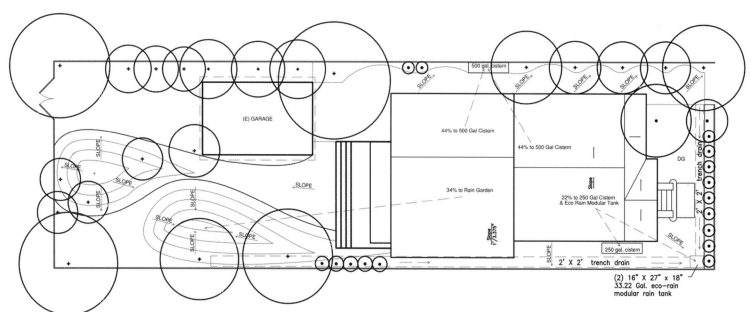

WATER MANAGEMENT

- 44 percent of roof runoff directed to 500-gallon cistern
- 34 percent of roof runoff directed to backyard rain garden
- 22 percent of roof runoff directed to 250-gallon cistern and EcoRain modular rain tank

architect and the plumber in tandem with the graywater engineer, contractor, and landscaper. The site was designed to allow water to permeate through the ground naturally or be directed into infiltration pits. The backyard is a formalized version of the natural world: aesthetically pleasing native plants both conserve water and provide sustenance for native critters. The home's graywater system pumps water to riparian trees and a crescent of banana plants.

The house highlights the efficiency of stormwater/graywater reuse and infuses elements of beauty into water-delivery systems. Two cisterns collect 750 gallons of rainwater from three different sources. The cisterns and their accessories (first flush diverter, rain chains, and downspouts) are positioned for functionality and visibility. One reservoir waters a fruit orchard; the other, itself a fish habitat, irrigates a flower garden. In the backyard, roof runoff passes over a waterwheel into a fountain; the fountain overflows into a planted swale.

In addition to reducing the footprint and environmental impact of her house, the architect strived to restore habitat for birds, bees, and butterflies and to create educational opportunities for the neighborhood and for visitors. The site is organized by habitat, access, and views and zoned into areas of native chaparral, riparian shrubs/trees, fruit orchard, flowers, berry patch, banana bed, and vegetable garden. Water is visible within each zone.

Duvivier, who has many favorite features throughout the house, found that acting as project manager as well as architect and owner was the biggest challenge. Many subcontractors wanted to work according to standard operating procedures, but the standard way, Duvivier discovered, is often at odds with the most environmentally responsible way. Persistence, hard work, and collaboration were the secret ingredients in overcoming these obstacles.

Quality Insulation Installation

The Quality Insulation Installation and Thermal Bypass Checklist Procedure is a process for confirming the quality of insulation and thermal-barrier installation in low-rise residential buildings. Following QII guidelines is required for participation in the California Energy Star Homes program.

Juanita Verde

Palm Springs, California
Architect: Eric Corey Freed, organicARCHITECT

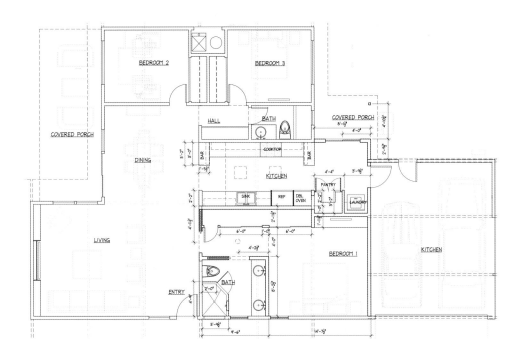

Modernism meets green in this Palm Springs remodel by Eric Corey Freed, author of, among other books, the bestselling *Green Building and Remodeling for Dummies*. Philip Johnson once described Freed as "one of the real brains of his generation." The clients, Chris Lucas and Paul McCreesh, principals of the Palm Springs firm GreenGuys Construction, were likewise familiar with all that would be needed for the monumental makeover of a fifty-year-old home. Lucas and McCreesh, Certified Green Building Professionals who lecture regularly at the College of the Desert, viewed their architect as a trusted source of knowledge when navigating the often overwhelming world of green homebuilding.

Freed's creative design honors the spirit of the original midcentury structure, a Southern

California Meiselman home with iconic butterfly roof built in 1959. He and the GreenGuys stripped away decades of neglect, restored the former glory, and added the latest in materials, energy efficiency, and healthy features. The Rat Pack and other stylish denizens of Palm Springs in its heyday would feel right at home. Says Freed, "I had a wonderful existing house with 'great bones' and great clients open to new ideas. The clients also happened to be green-minded and talented contractors."

The interior of the original home—small kitchen, tiny bathrooms, and a cramped master bedroom—was both reconfigured and restored. The team filled the space between the house and garage, gaining almost 250 square feet and creating a private area in the rear for

a grill and sun deck. The new and open allocation of spaces, inside and out, accommodates a more modern lifestyle.

The severe desert climate demanded a high-performance building. The original home had practically no insulation—a "mere film of aluminum foil," as the homeowners describe it—since it was planned as a winter getaway. The Green Guys filled the walls with a soy-based foam from BioBased Technologies that cuts cooling bills by 90 percent. Low-E double windows and six inches of cool foam on the roof add to the savings and comfort level.

Water is scarce in the desert, so the architect and owners opted for dual-flush toilets, ultra-

low-flow fixtures, and, outside, natural "desert-scaping." The house will save thousands of gallons of water each year. Finishes are up-to-date in function but faithful to the period of the house in appearance. Recycled glass from bottles and windshields was used in the IceStone countertops and the ModWalls subway tiles in the backsplash and shower.

Instead of traditional building materials, with formaldehyde, VOCs, and carcinogens, Freed, Lucas, and McCreesh chose healthy versions. Neil Kelly Cabinets, for instance, are made from no-added-formaldehyde Agriboard and low-VOC and no-added-formaldehyde glues, adhesives, and finishes.

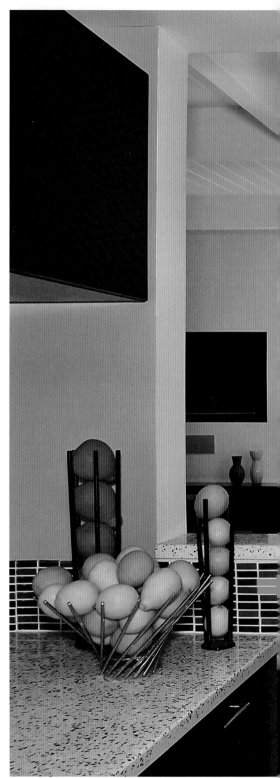

Certified Green Builders

The National Association of Home Builders designates as Certified Green Professionals builders, remodelers, and other industry workers who have mastered strategies for incorporating green-building principles into homes without increasing construction costs. Certified Green Professionals must complete NAHB coursework and have a minimum of two years of experience in the construction industry. Through a similar program, Build It Green offers accreditation as a Certified Green Building Professional.

Esther's Island Retreat

Nantucket County, Massachusetts
Architect: Hart Howerton

Off the western tip of Nantucket Island, on a tapering spit of sand and sea grasses, lies tiny Esther's Island, accessible only by boat. Despite the challenges of building on such a remote site, architect Hart Howerton has built a house there to LEED Gold standard. The client, a long-time Nantucket resident and owner of resort properties in coastal areas, purchased the ten-acre site to study environmentally sensitive building practices. The knowledge he gained at the Esther's Island house will be transferred to his company's other projects.

One of just three residences on the island, the home is a compound of four independent "cottages," each representing a room—living room/kitchen and three bedrooms. The individual components use energy more efficiently and generate social and secluded areas in the home. Combining the kitchen and living spaces also created efficiency in the design.

Inspired by the Nantucket attached-cottage vernacular, the individual living spaces open onto wide decks and covered porches. These transitional areas provide a strong connection between inside and outside and nearly double the compound's living spaces. But the local

vernacular was an aesthetic influence only. The retreat has been constructed with renewable materials including FSC-certified lumber, low-VOC paints, furnishings of natural and recycled materials, water-efficient fixtures, and an environmentally sensitive septic and leaching field system. The landscape consists of drought-resistant dune grasses and native flowering plants; turf is limited to small areas adjacent to the house. Irrigation is provided by captured rain-water stored in an underground cistern.

"Off the grid" was not just a philosophy for this Nantucket residence; it was a necessity. No utilities are available on Esther's Island, so all energy must be generated on site. Power is produced by means of renewable resources: photovoltaic solar array and five-kilowatt wind turbine for electricity and flat-panel solar thermal array for hot water.

The vertical-axis turbine, which spins like a barber's pole, is efficient in low wind, quieter and a better neighbor to birds than a conventional horizontal-rotor windmill, and has a minimal visual impact. A monitoring system tracks energy consumption and reports when stores fall low. Each of the cottages is an individual unit that can be closed off from the rest of the home and heated or cooled as necessary. High-efficiency appliances and lights and low-flow plumbing equipment were incorporated into the house.

Economy in both design and construction is pivotal in this sensitive environment. Construction waste was kept below 10 percent, and the volume of solid waste was reduced by chipping into mulch what could be incorporated into the soil. To mitigate the physical impact of the house, it rests on a raised structure supported by piles screwed into the ground. The screw

piles were installed with a small piece of machinery and can easily be removed from the earth, leaving the site undisturbed.

The structure is sheathed in FSC cedar shingles that will weather in the strong winds and salt spray off the ocean; on the interior walls of the new porch are salvaged shingles. Low-VOC paints and sealants were used inside the house, along with natural fibers and recycled materials. The living room fireplace, for example, was constructed of found stones and driftwood.

FSC-Certified

Established in 1993 in response to global deforestation concerns, the Forest Stewardship Council is an international not-for-profit organization that provides tools to promote responsible forest management to businesses and consumers. The organization sets standards for managing forests and certifies and labels forest products. FSC certification denotes a product that comes from a source that is environmentally responsible, socially beneficial, and economically viable.

Helenowski Residence

Chicago, Illinois
Architect: Mariusz Bleszynski

Jacek Helenowski, owner of Square 1 Precision Lighting in Chicago, has been involved in cutting-edge energy efficiency and renewable energy technologies for more than twenty years. He believes in the concept of "practice what you preach" and, in renovating this residence in Chicago's Edgebrook neighborhood, put his passion for and dedication to energy conservation and the environment on the line. His home is recognized not only as Chicago's greenest home but as a premier LEED-certified residence. According to LEED for Homes provider Alliance for Environmental Sustainability, it has achieved Platinum certification with one of the highest scores ever: 119 out of a possible 136 points. The house is also Energy Star certified and has earned three stars (the highest rating) from the Chicago Green Homes Program. In addition, the residence garnered a rating of thirteen on the HERS (Home Energy Rating System) Index (where zero indicates that a building uses no net purchased energy and one hundred represents the energy use of a standard American building) by using CFC-free soy-based foam insulation, renewable energy features, and ultra-efficient plasma-cold-cathode lighting.

Helenowski believes that building green is a whole-building, systematic approach to design and construction. He served as researcher, systems integrator, builder, and project manager for his home. Helenowski began his research, which was considerable, in 2000; four years later, he began seven years of construction, gutting and entirely rebuilding the house, mostly on nights and weekends. The project cost an astonishingly low $80 per square foot—a true example of affordable green building. Architect Mariusz

Cold-Cathode Lighting

Cold-cathode lamps have been used for years in laptop displays, photocopiers, and cell phones. Even some of the new flat-panel LCD television screens and monitors utilize proven and reliable cold-cathode technology. Recently, the technology has been adapted and applied to compact lighting products, which have an average life rating of twenty-five thousand hours. Due to its efficiency, cold-cathode fluorescent lighting technology has expanded into room lighting. Costs are similar to those of fluorescent lighting, but CCFLs have several advantages: the light is easier on the eyes, the bulbs turn on instantly to full output, and they are dimmable.

Bleszynski developed the working drawings and also performed the LEED certifications through the USGBC.

One of the first contemporary net-zero-energy residences in the United States, the home uses a host of renewable resources to produce as much energy as it consumes over the course of a year. A geothermal heating and cooling system uses the Earth's constant ground temperature to help heat the house in the winter and cool it in the summer. A multifuel pellet heater supplies supplemental heat. Three rows of photovoltaics on the roof and a vertical-axis wind turbine furnish energy.

The soybean-based foam insulation Helenowski selected for the roof provides an R-value of up to 90. Triple-paned wood windows with internal blinds further insulate the building envelope. Thermostats on the front windows (which face west) operate motorized blinds to help control heating and cooling. Excess heat from the geothermal HVAC system and passive solar thermal storage is directed to a home spa.

Naturally, Helenowski takes eco-friendly lighting seriously. The high LEED score could not have been achieved with compact fluorescent lights (which contain mercury) or LED lights (which contain arsenic), Helenowski says. His company's

plasma-cold-cathode lighting, which uses very little electricity, has a potential lifespan of more than eighty thousand hours, and is up to 300 percent more efficient than LEDs, made the difference. The rooms with plasma-cold-cathode lighting use about 0.4 watt of power per square foot. The residence also features a rotating hydroponic growing system, which uses plasma-cold-cathode lighting to produce a fresh crop of lettuce every four to six weeks. Helenowski has collaborated with renowned artist James Turrell on the latter's lighting installations; the artist selected the lighting for the house, including the changing color system for the home spa, and has designed an art piece for future installation.

Indoor air quality was fostered by no-formaldehyde MDF trim and doors, low-VOC paints, and clear coats in the finishes. Vegetable-oil-based flooring in the basement and a central open-tread stairway from the basement to the top level aid in natural air movement. The landscaping highlights native species, reducing irrigation needs, and a rainwater capture system collects water for the lawn and garden, reducing use of city water. Permeable, light-colored pavers on the driveway and walkways lessen water runoff; low-flow plumbing fixtures further conserve resources.

Helenowski took meticulous care to use reclaimed materials. On the exterior are a reclaimed copper roof with durable stitch-weld seams, reclaimed stone fragments, and concrete with fly ash. Inside, the owner focused on materials with recycled content. Drywall is made almost entirely from gypsum from coal-burning power plants in East Chicago. Ninety-two percent of dimensional lumber was either reclaimed from the original building or recut from a burned building in Chicago in a salvage operation that took a year and a half. The roof deck is covered in recycled tire rubber; elsewhere, a green roof offers vegetation. The balance of the roof is white to reflect the sun. Renewable bamboo flooring was installed in most rooms; the cabinets and basement bar are crafted from FSC-certified wood. More than 90 percent of construction waste was diverted from landfills.

Architect Bleszynski notes that Jacek Helenowski was highly motivated to realize the best green building possible according to the fundamental principle of ecological design—reuse and recycle first. "Ecologically sound construction is still an emerging art, which requires passion and leadership, and he supplied plenty of both," says Bleszynski.

Hix Island House

Vieques, Puerto Rico
Architect: John Hix Studios

Architect John Hix is acclaimed for his design of striking, energy-efficient buildings that are connected to nature. Perhaps the Canadian designer's most celebrated project is Hix Island House, a nineteen-room hotel on Vieques. It serves as Hix's home for much of the year, and it is also an eco-tourism destination of note. His comprehensive sustainable design strategy earned Hix Island House the first "Sustainable Tourism Facility" certification awarded by Puerto Rico Tourism and an Environmental Quality Award from the U.S. Environmental Protection Agency.

Vieques, a four-by-twenty-one-mile islet eight miles from the main island of Puerto Rico, is accessible only by ferry or short flight from San Juan, St. Croix, or St. Thomas. This unspoiled paradise of wild horses and secluded beaches was until recently virtually unknown, due in large part to the fact that up to 2003 much of the island was a bombing range for the U.S. Navy. Now Vieques is a fashionable Caribbean destination, full of trendy restaurants, art galleries, and increasingly posh hotels.

Hix Island House, a bucolic yet luxurious retreat of Zen-like elegance, is sturdily sculpted from reinforced concrete. Built over a twenty-one-year period, the hotel is characterized by clean and unadorned walls, massive support columns, infinity pools, and heavy louvered windows and steel security doors rather than panes of glass.

Hix says he studied local architecture to learn how to craft buildings that are beautiful yet acknowledge the climate of Puerto Rico. For the Hix Island House, he was inspired by the

R-Value

R-value is a measurement of thermal resistance—the ability of a material (generally a form of insulation) to resist heat transfer. The higher the R-value, the greater the insulating properties. Standard single-pane window glass has an R-value of less than one, while closed-cell polyurethane spray foam has an R-value of around six.

mammoth gray granite boulders scattered across Vieques. The huge stones blend with and are absorbed by the landscape yet are awe-inspiring when encountered on a steep grassy hillside or by a shimmering bay. Hix's creations are likewise at home in the landscape.

The hotel was built in a manner that might be called *wabi-sabi* (a Japanese aesthetic embracing transience and imperfection). Concrete block and reinforced concrete surfaced with plaster are hurricane-, earthquake-, and fire-proof. The unglazed windows offer guests a direct connection with the weather and the environment. The resort's stout concrete buildings with their solid steel doors and hefty wooden shutters have often served as safe harbors for neighbors and friends during hurricane season.

John Hix calls his approach to landscape design "gardening nature." He adds a limited number

of plants but primarily removes the under-growth from native species found on the site. This instant, low-maintenance landscape is at one with the surrounding countryside, or "nuestro campo," as Hix describes it.

The loftlike guestrooms are solar-powered and sited to take full advantage of cooling ocean breezes. Modernist decor and other stylish amenities entice design-conscious guests, while conservation-minded features appeal to those who like to "travel green." Solar panels augment the electricity and hot water; photovoltaic panels power the filter system for Hix Island House's two swimming pools—no commercial electricity is used. Graywater collected from showers and basins irrigates the guavas, bananas, papayas, and lemons on the property, further incorporating the resort into the cycles of nature.

Hix's latest project at the hotel complex is Casa Solaris, the first completely "off-grid" guesthouse in the Caribbean. Its six luxurious suites are fossil-fuel- and pollution-free. Like the main lodging, Casa Solaris relies on wind for cooling, solar hot water for outdoor showers, and photovoltaic solar cells for electricity. Yet here Hix has extended his eco-friendly vision to comprise water-saving appliances, improved composting systems, and zero use of electricity from the power grid.

The architect first explored off-grid, electricity-free designs as far back as the 1960s; Casa Solaris is thus the culmination of a lifetime spent pursuing truly green design. "There's something very satisfying about seeing it actually work more than five decades later," Hix says.

Caribbean Villa

Vieques, Puerto Rico
Architect: John Hix Studios

Donna Gorman and Roger Johansson discovered the unspoiled beaches and bucolic landscape of Vieques long before it became a fashionable tourist destination. They snatched up a pristine lot on the island's undeveloped south side, with a view over grassy hills and down to the sea, for a family getaway.

The couple had stayed at John Hix's Hix Island House on earlier visits to Vieques and had fallen in love with its design and style of living. Hix developed a low-maintenance vacation home that, like his resort, incorporates modern influences as well as the natural Caribbean landscape. The simple residence is constructed of low-maintenance, stormproof concrete with clean, resilient finishes. As at the Hix Island House, heavy steel doors and louvered metal windows are used instead of traditional doors and windows, lessening the separation between the natural environment and the home's inhabitants.

Gorman and Johansson requested a straight-forward floor plan: a single large living area and two bedrooms. They wanted a house that would encourage indoor-outdoor living, with outdoor showers and expansive verandas that fuse seamlessly with the interior of the house. To ensure that the hillside home had ample views of the ocean, Hix elevated the building almost a full story, creating storage space and room for two immense rainwater cisterns. Expansive southwest-facing floor-to-ceiling windows capture cool trade winds and panoramic sea views alike.

Because of expensive and sometimes unreliable island electricity, not to mention the plentiful sunshine, the Caribbean is an especially appropriate place for solar-powered homes. Hix called for sets of roof-mounted photovoltaic panels angled to capture the maximum level of solar energy. The sixteen solar panels charge twenty batteries. Two panels heat the household water; six power the swimming pool pump and filter system; and the remainder run lights, ceiling fans, and the few appliances the family requires.

Hix notes of his design philosophy that he considers the things found in nature more fascinating and beautiful than those that are fabricated by humankind. He also works to comprehend the forces that shape those natural things. Hix strives to make his buildings fit with nature and also to react to natural forces as though they were aspects of the natural world.

Off-Grid Solar Electric Systems

Solar electric systems not connected to an electric utility are called "off-grid" or "stand-alone" systems. The most common form of off-grid system stores solar-generated electricity in batteries for later use. While some off-grid homes use direct current appliances, most systems with battery backup use an inverter to convert the direct current electricity from the solar array to the alternating current used by most household appliances.

Ferrous House

Spring Prairie, Wisconsin

Architect: Johnsen Schmaling Architects

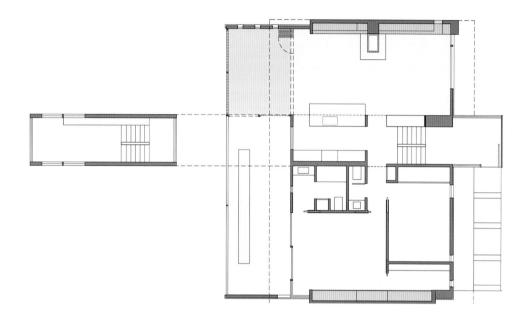

The Ferrous House is the sustainable reinvention of an end-of-life-cycle suburban home. The project offers a sensible alternative to the ordinary but environmentally irresponsible approach of "tear down and build bigger," illustrating how the bones of an outdated building can be reclaimed as the framework for a contemporary, precisely detailed dwelling—a case study for a resource-conscious suburban renewal.

Located in a subdivision west of Milwaukee, the existing 1,300-square-foot structure, a dark house with few windows, had fallen into disrepair. The clients wanted to reconfigure both the appearance and the spatial allocation of the house; at the same time, a limited construction budget and an attentiveness to the environment commanded the reuse of the existing foundations, main perimeter walls, and plumbing stacks. The interior was gutted and reorganized to create open, interconnected spaces. Linear cedar-clad storage boxes, containing built-in closet systems and living room cabinetry, cantilever over the edge of the building and add additional space without altering the original footprint of the house. A new shed roof, supported by a filigree of exposed metal and wood trusses, adds height to the living spaces and allows northern light to wash the inside of the house via a long band of translucent, aerogel-filled polycarbonate glazing.

In a carefully choreographed entry sequence, wide exterior stairs run along the front of the house and lead up to a small glazed porch. More stairs weave through the house, terminating in a small observatory above the new roof. The simple rectangular volume of the residence is wrapped on three sides by a steel rainscreen; as it weathers, the warm color of ferrous corrosion will echo the hues of farm equipment left on the area's abandoned pastures. In the back,

Green Building

Until fairly recently, a green building simply meant an energy-efficient building. Over time, the term has expanded in scope to include holistic approaches to sustainable materials and building methods; strategies to improve indoor air quality; and techniques that account for the embodied energy of materials, life-cycle costs of a building, and the recycling of used materials back into the building stream.

the steel wrapper extends beyond the edges of the building to shelter the sides of a south-facing patio and a screened porch, accessible from the living area through a retractable folding-glass-door system. In the summer, the living room expands into the porch, transforming into a "green lung" that naturally draws the cool breeze from the nearby woods.

Installed throughout the building are sustainable systems and materials, including low-VOC paints and stains, recycled steel, high-efficiency mechanical systems, Energy Star–rated windows, and locally sourced woods. A high-endurance VaproShield wall membrane and high-efficiency closed-cell expanding-foam insulation (sourced from agricultural byproducts to avoid the use of petrochemicals) comple-ment the perimeter rainscreen. The aerogel-filled polycarbonate clerestory has an R-value of 7, exceeding that of regular insulating glass by 90 percent and drastically minimizing the need for artificial light.

OS House

Racine, Wisconsin

Architect: Johnsen Schmaling Architects

Commissioned by a young family, the OS House is one of the first LEED Platinum homes in the Upper Midwest. The 1,900-square-foot residence demonstrates how a small, sustainable house built on a moderate budget can become a confident urban constituent.

Located in an old downtown neighborhood, the home occupies a narrow lot along Lake Michigan. Adjacent residences are opaque masses, but the OS House features expanses of glazing on the main level that allow for a visual connection between street and lake. The upper portion of the house is wrapped in a rainscreen composed of thin concrete panels suspended between pairs of horizontal steel channels. The resulting eight-inch-deep ventilated envelope offers superior protection from the elements.

The structure is organized along the north-south axis to take advantage of cool eastern lake breezes during the summer. High-performance, low-E, argon-filled operable windows throughout provide cross ventilation. A central staircase functions as a thermal chimney, allowing warmer air from the main level to escape through windows in the upper observatory. A large southern overhang minimizes solar heat gain in the summer while harnessing the sun's warmth in winter.

For most of the year, the cross ventilation furthered by the operable windows and the shallow building volume conditions the house. In the winter months, a dedicated outdoor air-supply system, in conjunction with a heat-recovery system, provides fresh air to the occupants. Low- and no-VOC paints and cabinetry minimize off-gassing and air pollutants inside the house.

The roof feeds rainwater into a groundwater percolation area via rain chains and drainage tiles and also into two large barrels, where it is used to water a vegetable garden. All plant material, selected and placed strategically to control erosion, is native and drought tolerant, requiring essentially no irrigation. Water conservation inside the house is promoted by a compact structured plumbing system with low-flow fixtures and an on-demand hot-water circulating pump.

Heating and cooling is provided by a geothermal ground-source heat pump with a vertical loop system. The envelope of the house is insulated with an agricultural-based closed-cell expanding-foam insulation, which yields R-values of 34 in the walls and 53 in the roofs. Innovative wood-framing techniques were deployed: two-stud corners avoid the fully blocked "cold" corner detail typically used in residential construction, and wall studs at twenty-four rather than sixteen inches on center decrease thermal bridging and increase the insulated surface area.

About 70 percent of the electric power consumed in the house is generated by a 4.2-kilowatt photovoltaic system; the system consists of PV laminates adhered to the roofing membranes as well as a freestanding array. In summer, excess power from the photovoltaic system feeds back into the grid. Hot water is generated by a solar hot-water panel that preheats the water, backed up by a tankless water heater. Insulated pipes and an on-demand pump distribute the hot water efficiently.

Materials were carefully selected based on durability and maintenance, healthy features, and environmental characteristics (sustainable, recycled, rapidly renewable). Preference was given to materials that could be locally or regionally sourced and manufactured, including the rainscreen panels, windows, lumber, tiles, plumbing fixtures, and pavers.

The framing reduced the amount of lumber by 30 percent, as compared to conventional construction, and lumber waste was limited to less than 10 percent. Clean wood recycling and a diversion-focused waste hauler together shrunk construction waste to almost nothing. Interior materials include sustainable bamboo flooring, locally fabricated casework with FSC-certified engineered wood veneers and no added urea-formaldehyde, and domestically made wall and floor tiles.

CFLs and LEDs

A conventional incandescent light bulb uses only 10 percent of the energy drawn to produce light; the remaining 90 percent is wasted as heat. Compact fluorescent lights can lower a lighting load by 75 percent compared to incandescent or halogen bulbs. Ten-thousand-hour-rated CFLs burned three to four hours a day can last seven years. Light-emitting diode lights have the improved efficiency of CFLs but can last more than fifty thousand hours. The useful life of LED lighting products is defined differently from incandescents or CFLs: LEDs typically do not burn out but experience lumen depreciation, where the amount of light decreases and may change in color.

Hacienda Ja Ja

Alamo Heights, Texas
Architect: Lake|Flato Architects

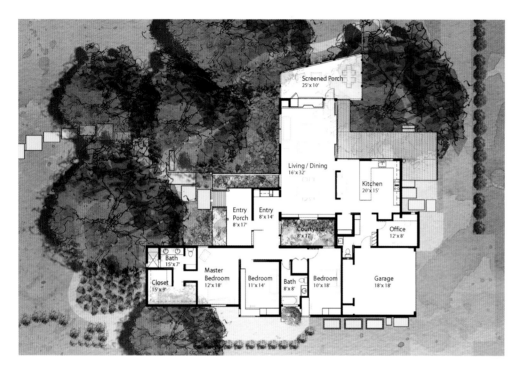

Homeowners Emily Sano and Gilson Riecken, a professional couple returning to Texas from San Francisco, had a well-defined concept for their residence. They were committed to a house that would fit into its natural surroundings both visually and environmentally, but they didn't want sustainable design aspects to dominate the feeling of the house. Bringing in natural light and incorporating an extensive art collection were key, as were exterior porches that would encourage engagement with activity on the street.

The couple fell in love with the live oak trees on a site in Alamo Heights, part of San Antonio. Nestled beneath the canopy, Hacienda Ja Ja is sited to preserve and protect the surrounding trees. The structure is also oriented to maximize natural ventilation and solar benefits.

The disposition of the rooms and the geometry of the roof are configured to avoid solar thermal gain during the summer and capitalize on passive solar heating during the winter. A high-efficiency, five-zone HVAC system augments these passive strategies and improves indoor air quality. Expanding spray-foam insulation protects the residence from air infiltration and additional heat gain. The carbon footprint of the residence is reduced by means of a seven-kilowatt photovoltaic array. In addition, solar thermal panels provide a majority of the residence's domestic hot water. Rainwater collected from the roofs is stored in a below-ground tank, supplanting household water for all landscape irrigation needs.

Various low-embodied-energy, rapidly renewable, and recycled building materials were used in the construction of Hacienda Ja Ja. The concrete in the foundation contains 30 percent fly ash. Locally sourced southern yellow pine constitutes the framing. Southern yellow pine lumber is typically dried to below 19 percent moisture content. Improved stability, minimal shrinkage, and exemplary nail-holding ability make it a preferred structural lumber. Locally harvested cedar siding wraps the exterior. Floors are surfaced in renewable, recycled-content cork and locally sourced stone, and Trex recycled-plastic-and-wood-fiber planking was used for the exterior decks.

Natural rather than mechanical ventilation is promoted in Hacienda Ja Ja, and zero-VOC construction adhesives and low-VOC paints, stains, and foam insulation also contribute to interior air quality. WaterSense-certified kitchen and bath fixtures reduce both electric and water bills. A six-thousand-gallon rainwater catchment irrigation system with moisture-sensor controller tends to the drought-tolerant native landscape (designed by Rialto Studio), and permeable exterior surfaces control runoff.

A residential energy management system reduces household energy use. A vampire, or "phantom," plug load is the level of energy a device consumes even while it appears to be turned off; "greenswitch" devices turn off all electronics not in use. LED and compact fluorescent lighting are used throughout the residence, as are Energy Star kitchen appliances.

The thoughtful implementation of environmentally conscious systems and strategies at Hacienda Ja Ja earned the residence LEED for Homes Platinum certification. In 2012, the first year of full occupancy, the house produced as much energy as it consumed. Shortly after the building was completed, the owners added an energy dashboard system to track energy use within the home, as well as daylight, humidity, and temperature monitors. These monitoring systems display real-time performance data, offering a detailed glimpse of household energy consumption.

Urea-Formaldehyde

Classified as a known human carcinogen, urea-formaldehyde has been linked to respiratory irritation and other health problems (watery eyes, wheezing and coughing, skin rash, nausea, difficulty breathing, and more); cancer risk increases when air concentrations exceed three to five parts per million. It is no longer used in insulation, as it once was, but it is still heavily employed as an adhesive resin in wood flooring and laminates. Sustainable forest products generally have little or no urea-formaldehyde.

Leon Springs Residence

Bexar County, Texas
Architect: Lake|Flato Architects

The 3,600-square-foot Leon Springs Residence is a sustainable home that celebrates the outdoors, offers energy efficiency, harvests rainwater, and accommodates a professional couple and their guests, both young and old. The home sits lightly on a sloping site, taking advantage of views and solar orientation. Exposed steel and limestone blend into the surrounding Texas landscape. The roofs slope with the site and direct rainwater to a collection system. Roof overhangs provide shading from the hot Texas sun, while a steel pergola and sun sails shelter the stone pool deck, which merges with the home's limestone walls.

Three primary volumes are configured to create several outdoor spaces where the clients enjoy morning coffee, outdoor meals, and relaxation. Other outdoor living spaces include porches with stunning views and fresh breezes off the master bedroom and the guesthouse. The homeowners frequently sleep in the screened porch by the bedroom.

Overall energy consumption is reduced with both passive and active strategies, and the house received LEED for Homes Platinum Certification. The residence minimizes its impact on the natural environment in many ways. All interior spaces incorporate daylighting and cross ventilation. Reducing reliance on artificial lighting decreases cooling loads and increases occupant comfort. Passive solar techniques utilize the sun's heat in winter and temper it in summer. These features, along with the use of expanding-foam insulation, minimize the need for mechanical heating and cooling. A twelve-kilowatt photovoltaic array produces electricity, and a ground-source heat pump provides efficient heating and cooling as well as most of the home's domestic hot water.

Regional and low-embodied-energy materials, such as locally sourced Lueders limestone veneer and mesquite flooring, dominate the Leon Springs Residence. Walls are framed with finger-jointed studs, which would normally be considered scrap lumber. The concrete foundation is composed of 30 percent fly ash. All millwork uses FSC-certified, no-added-urea-formaldehyde plywood, and paints and sealants are low- or no-VOC. An on-site recycling strategy diverted 88 percent of construction waste from landfills. Scrap materials were ground into mulch and distributed across the site.

Rainwater collected from the roofs is stored in two 8,500-gallon tanks. This harvested rainwater is filtered in several stages to provide the homeowners with potable water. Once the drought-tolerant plantings have been established (the landscape architect was Sarah Lake), the clients hope to have net-zero water use.

Geothermal Heat Pumps

Geothermal or ground-source heat pumps tap into the relatively constant temperatures of the Earth, which stay between 50 and 55 degrees Fahrenheit, for heating and cooling. Geothermal heat pumps circulate food-grade glycol antifreeze through pipes deep in the ground, pulling heat up in cold weather and transferring it back down in warm weather. Ground-source systems use a fraction of the energy of conventional HVAC systems and, according to the EPA, can cut cooling expenses by 50 percent and heating expenses by 70 percent.

Greenbridge

Chapel Hill, North Carolina

Architect: William McDonough + Partners

Greenbridge, a 215,000-square-foot mixed-use residential, office, and retail project in the vibrant college town of Chapel Hill, demonstrates smart suburban growth in action. The site, located between two existing town centers, discourages sprawl. Sensitive massing and orientation and an optimized use of regionally appropriate materials and resources enhance the client's vision of the project as a model for conscious living.

The first mixed-use residential project in North Carolina built to LEED Gold standards, Green-bridge is poised to be a catalyst for the region. The design highlights energy conservation, comfort, individual control, and adaptability. Roof surfaces are productive—they are used to grow plants and food, retain water, generate power, reduce the heat-island effect, and offer areas of play and rest.

Greenbridge accommodates ninety-seven one-, two-, and three-bedroom condominiums—fifteen are designated as affordable housing—in its two-, seven-, and ten-floor towers. The complex covers 1.5 acres and includes thirty-three thousand square feet of commercial and office space, plus two levels of underground parking.

Greenbridge was carefully situated in relation to the transit and infrastructure of the nearby town centers. Seventy-five percent of demolition and construction materials were reused and recycled on-site. The shape and massing optimize daylight in public spaces and apartments; in fact, sunlight penetrates all public areas, offices, and apartments via terraces and a large central courtyard.

For the interior, William McDonough + Partners specified Cradle to Cradle–certified and other environmentally responsible products. Filtered outside air rather than recycled building air is delivered to all units. An enthalpy wheel heat-recovery system is used for energy savings and comfort.

In the bathrooms are faucets and showerheads with low-flow aerators as well as dual-flush toilets. All cements, solvents, and sealants are low-VOC. The recycled Stonepeak porcelain tile was installed with no-VOC setting materials; this procedure satisfied several LEED requirements, including local manufacture (within a five-hundred-mile radius). North Carolina artisans supplied the cabinetry. Once too expensive to be used on such a wide scale, LED lighting is the main source of illumination throughout the building.

Green surfaces on three roof levels boast organic, low-growth carpets of vegetation, and recycled rubber pavers cover nineteen-thousand square feet of terraces. High-performance recycled glass was used in the floor-to-ceiling windows. Greenbridge provides bicycles for resident use, and a car-sharing program reduces traffic congestion. A comprehensive rainwater-harvesting system directs rainwater to below-grade cisterns.

Enthalpy Wheel Heat Recovery

An energy-recovery ventilation system, an enthalpy wheel transfers heat and humidity from one air stream to another. The enthalpy wheel reclaims useful energy from building air and applies it to incoming, fresh air. In warm weather, the system precools and dehumidifies the air; in cooler weather, it preheats and humidifies it. By preconditioning outdoor air, the system reduces the need for air conditioning and heating.

Make It Right Flow House

New Orleans, Louisiana

Architect: William McDonough + Partners

Founded by actor Brad Pitt in 2007, in the aftermath of Hurricane Katrina, Make It Right develops healthy homes, buildings, and communities for people in need. The group's philosophy is that energy-efficient, well-designed homes should be affordable and available to everyone. All Make It Right projects are LEED Platinum—certified and Cradle to Cradle–inspired.

The Flow House, William McDonough + Partner's contribution to the Make It Right program, is a duplex for displaced residents of the Lower Ninth Ward in New Orleans. A three-bedroom primary residence at the street is paired with a one-bedroom rental, or "granny unit," with an independent entrance toward the rear. Conceived as a series of outdoor rooms that extend and expand indoor living spaces, this home connects to views, neighbors, and the community while orchestrating and celebrating the movement of light, shade, air, and water.

The design combines and reimagines local architectural typologies such as the shotgun, camelback, and dogtrot. Open and continuous spaces provide direct connections between residents and generous exterior spaces. Wide sliding doors extend the living room out to the front porch, and upper bedrooms open onto exterior deck spaces that accommodate rooftop gardens, family gatherings, and open-air sleeping.

The duplex is composed of three prefabricated sixteen-foot-wide modular units. Wall and roof assemblies are metal structural insulated panels; foundations, exterior cladding, and millwork are wood. Windows and other prebuilt components may one day be returned to their manufacturers

and reconstituted into new products. Wood used for millwork will be FSC-certified, formaldehyde-free, and responsibly harvested; wood used for cladding, structural columns, and foundation piles will be naturally treated through a nontoxic acetalization process. Gypsum-free, mold-resistant, low-VOC drywall will finish interior walls. An integrated system of scuppers and cisterns collects water for household use. Photosynthetic roof surfaces generate energy through integrated thin-film photovoltaics and hot water through solar thermal hot-water tubes.

Cradle to Cradle

In 2002, Michael Braungart and William McDonough published *Cradle to Cradle: Remaking the Way We Make Things,* which called for a new industrial revolution based on nature. Included were specific details for improving life-cycle design beyond the reduce/reuse/recycle model. The Cradle to Cradle Certification program, founded in 2005 by McDonough Braungart Design Chemistry, assesses a product's safety in regard to humans and the environment as well as its design for future life cycles in five categories: material health, material reutilization, renewable energy use, water stewardship, and social responsibility.

The Visionaire

New York, New York

Architect: Pelli Clarke Pelli Architects

The Visionaire is the third of three green condominium towers designed by Pelli Clarke Pelli Architects for Battery Park City and developed by the Albanese Organization. The Solaire, completed in 2003, was the first residential high-rise to attain a LEED Gold rating. The Verdesian, completed in 2006, received LEED Platinum certification, as did the Visionaire, completed in 2008. The mixed-use development includes 250 condominiums, a four-thousand-square-foot organic market, and the headquarters for the Battery Park City Parks Conservancy.

The thirty-five-story tower features a distinctive curved glass facade. Its slim profile reduces shadows cast on the surrounding area. The most visually expressive contribution to energy efficiency is the high-performance envelope—principally a terra-cotta rainscreen curtain wall with reflective low-E insulated glass.

During construction, half of the budget for building materials went to locally harvested products; 20 percent of materials were manufactured within five hundred miles of New York City. The terra-cotta screens, insulated glass, and thermally broken aluminum framing give rise to an exterior envelope with an R-value of 20. The Visionaire boasts on-site geothermal heat pumps, four thousand square feet of photovoltaic fuel cells, and a microturbine that generates electricity with the waste heat from the combustion used to heat the building's domestic water.

Occupant health and satisfaction greatly influenced the design. All air is fresh, not recycled through the building, and 40 to 45 percent of light comes from daylight. Sustainable technologies—plantings, permeable and highly reflective paved surfaces—are installed over 70 percent of the surface of the roof. The roof thus reduces

Cool Roof

Cool roofs, available for both commercial and residential buildings, fall into three broad categories: those made from inherently cool roofing materials, those covered with a solar-reflective coating, and those planted with vegetation. While cool roofs are often thought to be white, they come in a variety of colors and materials. Dark cool-roof pigments are less reflective than light colors, but they can still save energy over standard paints. Under LEED standards from 2009, to achieve the credit in this area, at least 75 percent of the surface of a roof must use materials with a solar-reflective index of at least 78. The credit can also be achieved by planting a green roof on at least 50 percent of the surface area or by installing a cool roof and vegetated roof in combination.

stormwater runoff and the heat-island effect while at the same time providing a recreation area for residents. The plantings also insulate the building.

In addition to the solar panels, which are integrated into the curtain wall, the building features a high-efficiency air-filtration system and wind-generated power. A water-treatment system recycles graywater for a cooling tower for the HVAC system. Five thousand gallons of recycled water are stored for irrigation of the rooftop garden.

The apartment interiors were devised by green interior designer Tim Button of Stedila Design. Kitchens showcase river-washed absolute granite countertops, glass backsplashes, renewable bamboo cabinets, and rift-cut oak flooring harvested according to FSC standards. All paints, adhesives, and sealants are environmentally friendly. Additional green amenities at the Visionaire include an indoor pool and Jacuzzi that are sanitized with ultraviolet light, greatly reducing the need for chlorine. The building also features bicycle storage and a charger for electric cars.

Ocean Avenue Residences

Oakland, California
Architect: Siegel & Strain Architects

The Ocean Avenue Residences are a pair of "book-matched" compact houses in northwest Oakland. Originally on the site—two legal but substandard lots—was a large, early-twentieth-century home that was destroyed by fire. The owner/contractor wanted to offer the community generously proportioned, sustainable, and comfortable homes.

The residences are located within a transitional area of Oakland. Six-story housing projects are rapidly growing along the main thoroughfare, San Pablo Avenue, dwarfing the early-twentieth-century residential areas on either side. The owner inaugurated this project in part to reknit the fragile fabric of this street—one block west of San Pablo Avenue—by providing a link between the apartment/condo blocks and the single-family houses. The owner/contractor also wanted to acknowledge the even smaller lots and houses on Peabody Lane to the north. The two 1,500-square-foot, two-story residences maximize living space while minimizing footprint and also provide significant outdoor space.

The tight zoning envelope and modest budget dictated simple but individuated designs. The two buildings are slightly offset, enhancing their privacy from one another. The rectangular volumes are clipped at opposite corners.

The sawtooth roof provides surfaces suitable for photovoltaic panels (and in fact is prewired), should the homeowners decide to install them. The roof form also draws light down to the lower floor, provides stack ventilation via double-height spaces, and offers colorful visual interest on both interior and exterior.

On the ground floors are living/kitchen/dining areas and double-height stair cores with half baths. Upstairs are two bedrooms and two baths. Sustainable features include drought-tolerant landscapes, high-fly-ash concrete with integrated radiant heating, efficient framing with recycled blown-in insulation, dual-glazed windows and doors, reclaimed fir siding at the core, and cement-fiber siding at the exterior. Among the green products are recycled glass tiles, recycled countertop material, bamboo flooring, low-VOC paints, and permeable paving. Exterior sunshades protect south-facing windows.

Every effort was made to create expansive spaces (nine-foot ceilings, double-height spaces) within the modest footprint; utilize durable, high-quality materials; and include family-sized storage and play areas. Efficient and healthy, the matched houses are also open, light-filled, and connected to spacious yards.

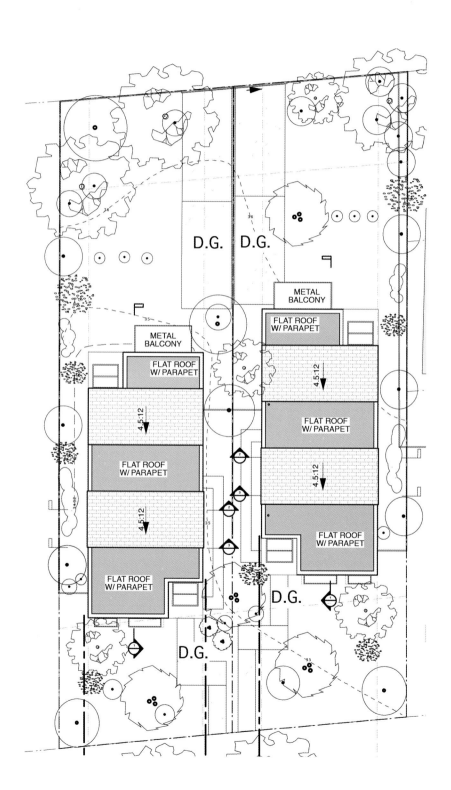

LEED for Homes

LEED for Homes, implemented in 2007, is a rating system for the design, construction, and operation of green homes. Developed by the U.S. Green Building Council, LEED-H awards points in eight categories of building practices and materials and eco-friendly product choices: innovation and design, locations and linkages, sustainable sites, water efficiency, energy and atmosphere, materials and resources, indoor environmental quality, and awareness and education. LEED-H was preceded by the LEED for Homes Program Pilot Rating System, which evaluated the rating system in terms of real-world application and promotion of green building practices in new homes.

Wine Creek Road Residence

Healdsburg, California
Architect: Siegel & Strain Architects

This small vacation house for a family of four interacts with its site in an understated but compelling way and at the same time expresses its sustainable values. The straightforward, inexpensive structure establishes an easy flow from inside to outside and fits effortlessly into the landscape. The residence has received several awards for environmental and sustainable design, including a Sustainable Residence Merit Award from AIA San Francisco and an AIA National COTE (Committee on the Environment) Top Ten Green Project Award.

The house sits in a grove of trees situated at the top of a sloping meadow. In this position it captures views across the large open area and is also protected from the hot afternoon sun. The main volume follows the contours of the site; two reverse-gable shed bays extend from the house up and down the slope. The living room bay looks out to the meadow and valley below, and the kitchen bay opens to views up the steep hillside behind. A simple gabled roof spans the residence. In the center is a dogtrot, or breezeway, that divides living and sleeping

Straw-Bale Construction

Straw-bale construction is an ancient building technique that employs bundles of straw (usually wheat, rice, rye, or oat straw) both as structural elements and as an insulator. The bales are typically encased in cement, adobe, or earth. Advantages of straw-bale construction are its renewable quality, relatively low cost, ready availability, and naturally fire-retardant and highly insulating properties (due to the thickness of the bales and the inherent dead air space among the fibers). Straw-bale construction is best suited to warm, dry climates because of its susceptibility to rot.

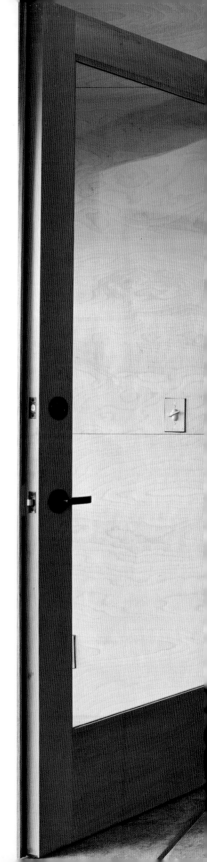

portions of the house. This outdoor living room is the heart of the Wine Creek Road Residence.

The house has a multitude of green features. Most of the exterior walls are constructed of straw bales with deep-set windows. The thickness of these walls is exposed at the dogtrot, where the protruding ends of the bales hold the plywood-veneer walls in place. The color scheme is an "anti-Tuscan" gray on gray accented by mahogany windows and doors.

Natural ventilation, superior insulation, and thermal mass keep the building cool during the hot summers. The thin building section, dogtrot, and arrangement of windows maximize opportunities for airflow. The high-performance, low-tech straw-bale building envelope—along with cellulose insulation, the thermal mass of the interior plaster walls, and the concrete floor—keeps the house cool through the hottest part of the day. Roof framing at twenty-four inches on center allowed for additional insulation and reduced thermal bridging.

Windows are wood, minimizing heat transfer, and double-glazed with low-emissivity glazing. A highly efficient water heater provides radiant floor heating. These measures resulted in a design that keeps the building cool except during the hottest hours of the hottest days. The owners chose energy-efficient, low-water-use appliances.

The residence surpasses California energy standards by more than 25 percent, despite the large amount of glazing. All of the building products, including sustainably harvested wood and recycled glass countertops, were selected for environmental performance and durability as well as for aesthetics.

Wilke-Duffy House

Bend, Oregon
Architect: Stillwater Dwellings

For some would-be green homeowners, a remote building site presents a daunting challenge. In addition to logistical hurdles, including exceptionally high construction costs—materials, workers, and equipment all must be transported to the site—owners are obliged to consider the effect on the surroundings. A new generation of sustainable prefabricated homes has greatly reduced these obstacles.

Clients Robert Duffy and Karen Wilke turned to Stillwater Dwellings for a house in the high desert of central Oregon; the site is characterized by expansive views of the Cascades. Stillwater founder Matthew Stannard believes the key to sustainability is energy frugality. All of the homes designed by his firm feature an ultra-tight, energy-saving exterior envelope, high-efficiency space- and water-heating systems,

and Energy Star appliances. Exterior walls are framed in 2x6s and incorporate high-performance foam insulation, producing an R-value of 20. Roofs, which utilize the same system, have an R-value of 50. The design and specification process focuses on mitigating environmental impact, and the fabrication system reduces waste by up to 50 percent in comparison to site-built homes.

All Stillwater homes have a signature butterfly roofline, interior light shelves to reflect daylight from clerestory windows, exterior "visors" for shading the facade, and steel-plate entry canopies. A standing-seam metal cool roof reflects over 30 percent of the sun's rays, and large overhangs assist with passive cooling. Efficient layouts emphasize indoor/outdoor living and entertaining.

The residences designed by Stillwater include numerous sustainable features: low-VOC paints, dual-flush toilets, natural wool carpeting, prefinished/engineered eco-friendly micro-strip birch hardwood, and natural linoleum flooring. Other green components are the heavily insulated walls, ceilings, and floors and high-efficiency windows with argon gas and a low-E film. Quartz slab countertops with recycled content are installed in the bathrooms.

A typical Stillwater home is composed of three to five modules—the Wilke-Duffy House has six. The modules are 96 percent complete when they arrive at the site: plumbing, electric, fixtures, cabinets, flooring, and wall coverings are already installed. Cranes lift the modules into position in a single day, and the final work is a simple matter of bolting the home to the foundation, connecting utilities, and finishing the joints between modules. The homes are ready for move-in in as little as three weeks after delivery.

Zero Impact House

North Easton, Massachusetts

Architect: Maryann Thompson Architects

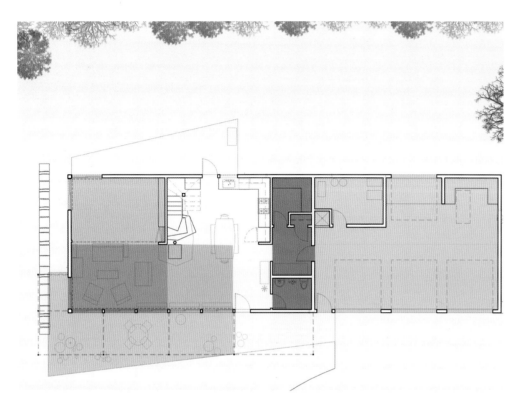

Embodied Energy

Although there are no universally accepted values for measuring embodied energy, it is deemed the sum of all the energy needed to manufacture a product, as if that energy were still "embodied" in it. Embodied energy may be considered either the energy expended in creating an item or the amount of carbon dioxide produced by its manufacture; the standard is applied to the entire life cycle, including raw material extraction, transport, manufacture, assembly, installation, deconstruction, and disposal. The LEED program considers the embodied energy of a building material one measure of a structure's environmental impact.

Although this simple and refined contemporary residence sits within a conventional suburban development, the densely wooded lot and adjacent conservation lands belie the setting. The siting of the house, deep within the 5.5-acre property down a nine-hundred-foot driveway, fosters a genuine connection with the landscape as well as a sense of seclusion and privacy.

The clients, one of whom is an environmental lawyer, requested an approach that was sensitive to the environment but also to the limited budget. The house responds to its surroundings, requires little maintenance, employs naturally occurring materials, and facilitates an informal lifestyle. The architectural form is deliberately straightforward—a simple box adorned with an asymmetrical roof line. In summer months, the asymmetrical roof shields the upstairs rooms from the intense sun. Open, light-filled public spaces for entertaining are adjacent to private spaces; every area of the three-thousand-square-foot house is connected, visually or physically, to the woodlands.

Numerous common-sense sustainable practices were incorporated into the residence, which has been certified LEED Silver under the LEED for Homes Program Pilot Rating System. The house is situated at the far end of an open meadow, allowing maximum solar exposure along its southern face, the principal facade. This orientation optimizes the solar energy production of three hundred square feet of

photovoltaic panels on the roof. Connection to the power grid assures the residents access to an emergency power source and enables them to sell unutilized energy resources to their local supplier. Expansive windows along the south front of the house take full advantage of the path of the sun over the course of the year. Small windows at the north side limit heat loss during long New England winters.

During the winter months, when the sun is low in the sky, abundant natural light is admitted into the public spaces and upstairs bedrooms, opening the house to solar gain. A fourteen-inch-thick concrete slab with a weathered bronze stain supplies substantial thermal mass, capturing solar heat from the south-facing windows during the day and slowly releasing it at night to heat the home. A central staircase with open risers allows free air flow to the three second-story bedrooms. Two pellet stoves and this efficient passive solar heating system satisfy heat requirements; in fact, the heating on the first floor is so efficient that the upstairs stove has yet to be used. The home is super insulated, boasting R values of 30 for the walls and 60 for the roof. Cross ventilation and ceiling fans eliminate the need for central air conditioning; windows carefully sited at the top of the stair create a stack effect, drawing hot air up and out of the home. A Mylar "solar curtain" along the south facade blocks the sun from heating the concrete slab in the warmer months.

Architect Maryann Thompson incorporated recycled and energy-efficient materials, always with an eye to cost considerations, including a recycled-tire-rubber roofing system that mimics the look of slate tiles; reclaimed hardwood cabinetry, casework, and flooring materials; recycled glass tiles; and thermally efficient windows. Homeowner Kyla Bennett was actively involved in the planning and construction of the home. She helped select many of the eco-friendly products, such as clay plaster that was applied to the walls instead of paint and sustainable bamboo strand flooring in the upstairs rooms. Unlike classic bamboo flooring, which is cut into strips and laminated, strand flooring is processed and compressed into dense logs. These logs are sliced for harder and denser flooring and plywood. The fiber-cement lap siding, which clads the house, has the look of wood clapboard but is longer lasting and rot resistant. It also requires less paint and maintenance than wood siding.

EnV

Chicago, Illinois
Architect: Valerio Dewalt Train Associates

The formula for residential life in an urban setting—boxy forms; predictable finishes, features, and planning concepts—has been evolving for decades. EnV, a new apartment tower in Chicago, avoids that template, proposing a design aligned with the current paradigm of urban life in which home, work, and leisure time are mingled.

The building is composed not as a single mass but as a series of glass panels that intersect and overlap to define the boundaries of the exterior form. Suspended from the building's concrete frame, these panels appear to be almost weightless. Some of the glass panels cantilever over the surrounding streets, defining glass-enclosed balconies.

Within EnV, glass surfaces are juxtaposed with other materials. The contrast between the materials accentuates their individual attributes. Muscular concrete columns stand in the apartments and common spaces. The use of post-tensioned concrete minimizes the number of structural columns; exterior columns are eliminated completely. Perforated metal panels wrap the base of the building in an industrial iconography that recalls Chicago's nineteenth-century "L" trains; one line, in fact, runs along the building.

The 390,000-square-foot building comprises 249 apartments—studio, one-bedroom, and two-bedroom units—and 30,000 square feet of retail. The seventh floor and the top floor are devoted to common areas. Most of the square footage within the apartments is given over to great rooms that take advantage of the views.

EnV has achieved a Certified rating from LEED. Among the sustainable components incorporated into the building are green roofs (approximately 5,500 square feet planted with native or adaptive plantings); low-VOC paints, adhesives, coatings, and carpet; and conservation strategies that reduce water consumption by 22 percent and energy consumption by 15 percent. The residential units feature bamboo floors, Energy Star refrigerators, and energy-efficient washers and dryers. Other eco-friendly aspects include high-efficiency lighting, comprehensive recycling programs, a no-smoking policy, and proximity to public transportation.

Fly Ash

Concrete was first produced in ancient Rome by mixing volcanic ash and lime. Portland cement, an essential component in modern concrete, is typically manufactured by heating limestone and clay at very high temperatures. Its production is extremely energy intensive and a major contributor of greenhouse gases. However, when fly ash, a waste byproduct of generating coal-powered electricity, is added to the concrete mix, the amount of Portland cement required can be drastically reduced.

Seneca House

Sarasota, Florida
Architect: Searl Lamaster Howe
Co-Architect: Valerio Dewalt Train Associates

Permeable Surfaces

Permeable surfaces allow rainwater to percolate into the ground; impermeable solid surfaces force water to run off. In addition to reducing runoff, permeable surfaces trap suspended solids and filter pollutants from the rainwater, improving groundwater quality and recharging the water table. Permeable surfaces used in construction include porous asphalt and concrete surfaces, concrete pavers with unsealed space between, polymer-based grass pavers, porous turf, gravel, plastic grids, and geocells.

This 2,500-square-foot LEED Platinum residence is composed of two intersecting forms: a masonry volume that defines the principal mass of the building and a horizontal plane, or terrace, that is supported on narrow masonry columns. Most windows in the masonry mass face north or south; all south-facing windows are shaded, while east- and west-facing windows are sheltered by the form of the house itself. The terrace supports an elevated pool at the main level of the house and covers the car park and defines the entry to the residence at grade.

The interior plan of the masonry volume is divided in half by an east-west wall, which acts as the backbone of the house. On the main living level, the area to the south of this wall is a great room; to the north are private sleeping and bathing areas. At grade, the mechanical room, the focus of all the technology in the house, occupies the area to the south of the wall; private rooms take up the space to the north.

Early in the design process the team gathered to develop strategies for integrating sustainable features into the building. As a result, the different systems work together to make the whole more efficient. For instance, shade for much of the south-facing glass is cast by solar collectors on the roof.

Those solar collectors absorb the energy of the sun to heat domestic hot water; any surplus is used to heat the pool. A five-kilowatt photovoltaic array powers the home fully for the six

weeks of the year it is occupied. The roof is designed to accommodate another five-kilowatt array; like the exterior walls, the roof is light in color, reflecting solar heat and keeping the interiors cooler.

An extensive rainwater harvesting system collects stormwater from the site. Three storage tanks capture all runoff from the roof. The water is filtered, treated with ultraviolet light, and used for both potable water and landscape irrigation (potted plants only). As required by the county, the system is backed up with a well and a reverse osmosis treatment system.

Crushed seashells pave walks and drives throughout the site. This permeable surface minimizes rainwater runoff. Landscaping, by Terrascape Landscape Architects of Sarasota, strategically locates native vegetation to eliminate the need for irrigation. Forty percent of the site was maintained in its natural state.

Wherever possible, material selection focused on products that were recycled (aluminum windows) or required little processing (stone countertops). "Finished" surfaces were generally avoided; concrete floors, for instance, were polished but have no chemical coating. These strategies both reduce cost and save energy. Low-VOC products improve indoor air quality by reducing the vapors and chemicals that are produced as materials off-gas. All plumbing fixtures are highly efficient, and all appliances are Energy Star–rated. During the construction process, material usage and recycling was a center of attention; 92 percent of all job waste was recycled.

UCSD Rita Atkinson Residences

La Jolla, California
Architect: Valerio Dewalt Train Associates
Interior Architect: Searl Lamaster Howe

Richard Atkinson and his wife, Rita, are legendary members of the University of California, San Diego community. Richard Atkinson was the chancellor of the university for fifteen years and then president of the UC system. To recognize the couple's $7.5 million donation to UCSD, the university named this graduate student housing facility for Rita Atkinson.

Rita Atkinson brings together the natural environment, sustainable construction practices, and sophisticated technologies. As a work of architecture it both follows and leads, respecting the overall campus plan. Two L-shaped wings, one nine stories and the other seven stories, nest together to form a three-sided courtyard. A grove of eucalyptus trees to the west creates an entry for the building. At the fourth level of the nine-story wing, the shape of the building changes to define a series of green roofs. Three-dimensional sculpting visually connects the building to the site.

A post-tensioned concrete frame is used as the structure of the building. In accordance with the principles of green building, the concrete is used as the final finish wherever possible. The concrete slabs were polished to become the finished floors, and the underside of the slabs became the finished ceilings. The plan minimizes the gross area of the building. Every switch, outlet, data point, plumbing fixture, cabinet, door, and sprinkler head was designed to reduce the amount of material required. The savings realized in a single room were multiplied 224 times when applied to the building as a whole.

Natural ventilation was incorporated through-out the residential building. In the corridors, outside air louvers draw air into the building; exhaust vents are connected via ventilation ducts to roof-mounted fans. These exhaust fans continually draw the inside air out. Low-flow toilets, lavatories, showerheads, and kitchen faucets contribute to a 30 percent reduction in water use.

Recycling has been made as convenient as pos-sible for the occupants of the building. Recycling centers are provided near each elevator lobby. These recycling centers offer a trash chute with a diverter to deliver trash and recyclables to the correct bins. Recyclables are transported to a materials recovery facility where they are sorted and marketed.

A combination of roof surfaces reduces the heat-island effect. Most of the building's upper roofs, as well as several other roofed areas, are covered in a material with a very high solar-reflective index, a measure of a roof's ability to deflect solar heat. In addition, a large green roof is planted with sedums, which provide good ground cover with only a shallow root system. The green roof system sits atop the roof assembly, which incorporates insulation beneath a waterproof membrane. Water that passes through the growing medium (mostly dirt) is strained and then collected by means of a filter fabric/drainage panel.

The residential facility benefits from UCSD's commitment to conscientious building techniques and sustainable programs. The university both purchases green power and produces its own. Solar panels provide one megawatt of energy, and a 2.8-megawatt fuel cell is powered by waste methane gas. All LEED-accredited buildings, including LEED Gold–certified Rita Atkinson, have a sufficient amount of energy produced by means of green methods and also offset the energy consumed by all buildings, new and old, across campus.

Urban Heat Island

An urban heat island is a metropolitan area that is considerably warmer than the neighboring rural areas. The temperature difference is usually larger at night than during the day, because buildings block surface heat from radiating into the cooler night sky. The main source of the UHI effect is alteration of the land surface by urban development: materials such as concrete, brick, stone, and asphalt absorb and retain heat. Waste heat produced by human activity is also a contributing factor. UHIs decrease air quality by increasing the production of pollutants, such as ozone, and decrease water quality as warmer waters flow into area streams, stressing their ecosystems. The heat-island effect can be diminished by green roofs and light-colored surfaces.

Berkeley Bungalow

Berkeley, California
Architect: Chris Parlette, WA Design

Architect Chris Parlette's childhood love of nature and technology has grown into a professional interest in sustainability and renewable energy. Since joining WA Design in 1993, he has translated that interest into integrating green technology, materials, and practices into nearly every project.

Parlette's own residence was originally an unsightly prewar bungalow in Berkeley. The architect set out to make the boxy, dark house more livable and also to incorporate a long list of sustainable features. He doubled the square footage by adding a second story, and he installed high-performance, low-E glass on the south and east sides of the structure. On the south, the glazing substantially increases daylighting and passive solar potential; on the east, it captures dramatic views of Mount Tamalpais and San Francisco Bay. A section of the roof cantilevers to shade the south face during the summer months.

Although Parlette gutted most of the existing structure, he saved a large portion of a previous kitchen remodel and also the original wood ceiling, living room beams, and fireplace. Recycled Douglas fir beams in the new ceiling upstairs share a sense of continuity with the beams downstairs. Parlette notes that wood reclaimed from old buildings is both stronger and more stable than most modern lumber. Other sustainable strategies included a building-integrated recycling center, drought-tolerant landscaping, and permeable concrete pavers that allow rainwater to reach the soil, dramatically reducing stormwater runoff.

Icynene spray-foam insulation is used above the ceilings. Spray-foam insulation can be injected into walls, ceilings, floors, crawlspaces, and attics; unlike insulation batts, it acts as an air barrier.

A 95-percent-efficient furnace and an outside-air intake promote improved indoor air quality.

Sustainable interior materials include bamboo flooring, recycled-content flooring, a recycled carpet pad underneath the wool carpet, and custom concrete-and-recycled-plastic counter-tops in the bathrooms. Cabinets in the master bedroom and bathroom have also been built from readily renewable bamboo. Interiors were finished with Benjamin Moore Eco Spec low- or no-VOC paint. A Rinnai tankless water heater and an Energy Star refrigerator and dishwasher reduce electricity needs. On the exterior, Trex recycled-plastic-and-wood-fiber composite was used for the window trim, decking, and land-scape edging.

An operable skylight on the upper level brings light into the residence and also creates a "stack effect," or thermal chimney, drawing air up through the house on hot days. In cooler weather, the sun warms a slate floor in the master bathroom; the floor slowly releases the stored heat throughout the day. Strategically placed windows increase natural cross ventilation.

Parlette believes that energy efficiency com-bined with active and passive solar strategies has produced a house that is net zero with regard to electricity. A 3.2-kilowatt photovoltaic array on the roof generally produces more electricity than he uses. In Berkeley, as in many locales, the utility company is required to pay or credit the homeowner for excess electricity sent back to the grid from such a system.

Net Metering

Net metering is an electricity policy for consumers with renewable energy systems. Under net metering, a system owner receives retail credit for at least a portion of the electricity generated. Most electricity meters accurately record both energy in and energy out; excess electricity production may be "banked" for future use. However, the rules regarding the duration and value (retail or wholesale) of the banked credits vary significantly from state to state.

Stinson Beach House

Marin County, California
Architect: David Stark Wilson, WA Design

Natural Ventilation

Natural ventilation—often through
open windows, skylights, and attic
vents—uses air movement to cool
a home. Since moving air speeds the
evaporation of perspiration, residents
feel cooler at warmer temperatures.
Carefully positioned openings on
opposite sides of a building encourage
cross ventilation. Cross ventilation can
be improved by means of a thermal
chimney, or "thermosiphon": operable
windows and skylights at the lowest
and highest points in the structure.
Ventilated attics are cooler than
unventilated ones by about 30 degrees
Fahrenheit, and solar-powered attic
vents require no external power.

It took years for architect David Stark Wilson
and his wife, Stacia, to find a south-facing lot in
Marin County suitable for the energy-efficient
beach home they dreamed of building. The site
they finally purchased is in the small coastal
town of Stinson Beach. Both budget realities
and zoning regulations limited their design to
1,400 square feet. Wilson resolved to create in
this small home the spacious feeling of a much
larger building, conceptualizing the regional
modernist design in inches rather than feet.

A great room offers an inviting and expansive
living space for gatherings of family and friends;
bedrooms are scaled back to provide little
more than sleeping space. Cement board and
an aluminum-zinc-alloy-coated steel called Gal-
valume, which mirrors the ubiquitous corru-
gated barns along Highway 1, generate a sturdy
yet cost-effective exterior.

The owners developed several clever solutions
to reduce clutter and maximize open living
areas. Custom pieces of furniture include
banquettes with hidden storage space and a
wheeled coffee table that can be rolled out of
the way to clear floor space for yoga. Clerestory
windows provide ample sunlight, and steel-cable
railings enhance the feeling of openness.

Wilson built sustainable design into the residence through various materials and systems,
including open-cell insulation, concrete floors,
natural ventilation, and recycled resources.

The ceiling consists of reclaimed planks of Douglas fir from a hundred-year-old university gymnasium. A dining table was crafted from an elm tree salvaged from a Palo Alto parking lot.

The south-facing roofline is ideal for extensive photovoltaic and solar thermal systems. These arrays, which satisfy all energy requirements of the home, cost about $40,000 but save $250 or more a month. The ocean breezes and mild climate of Stinson Beach eliminated the need for air conditioning. Sunlight enters deep into the home through windows on the southern facade; during the day, it is absorbed by the concrete floor, and at night it radiates back out.

Resources

Green Building Products and Organizations

American Forest and Paper Association
www.afandpa.org

American Institute of Architects Committee on the Environment
www.aia.org
network.aia.org/CommitteeontheEnvironment/Home

American Society of Landscape Architects
www.asla.org

APA—The Engineered Wood Association
www.apawood.org

BuildingGreen.com
www2.buildinggreen.com

Build It Green
www.builditgreen.org

Congress for the New Urbanism
www.cnu.org

Consortium for Research on Renewable Industrial Materials
www.corrim.org

Energy and Environmental Building Association
www.eeba.org

Energy Star
www.energystar.gov

Environmental Building News
www.BuildingGreen.com

Forest Stewardship Council
www.fscus.org

Global Green USA
www.globalgreen.org
www.treehugger.com

Green Building Advisor
www.greenbuildingadvisor.com

Green Building Supply
www.greenbuildingsupply.com

Green Point Rated
greenpointrated.com

***GreenSource* Magazine's Resource Guide**
greensource.construction.com/products

Healthy Building Network
www.healthybuilding.net

High Performance Buildings Database, U.S. Department of Energy
eere.buildinggreen.com

LEED For Homes
www.leedforhomes.org

***Natural Home and Garden* Magazine's Resource Guide**
www.naturalhomeandgarden.com/resource-guide.aspx

Residential Energy Services Network Energy Rater
www.resnet.us/energy-ratings

Square 1 Precision Lighting, Inc.— Cold Cathode Lighting
www.sq1pl.com

Sustainable Buildings Industry Council
www.sbic.org

U.S. Green Building Council
www.usgbc.org

USGBC Green Home Guide
www.greenhomeguide.com

Renewable Energy Industry Groups

American Society of Heating, Refrigeration, and Air Conditioning Engineers
www.ashrae.org

American Solar Energy Society
www.ases.org/solar

Energy Efficiency & Renewable Energy Clearinghouse Network
www.eren.doe.gov

Hydronic Radiant Heating Association
Tel: 530.753.1100

National Association of State Energy Officials
www.naseo.org

National Renewable Energy Laboratory
www.nrel.gov

Solar Energy Industries Association
www.seia.org

Sustainable Buildings Industry Council
(see above)

Other Organizations

Center for Renewable Energy & Sustainable Technology
www.crest.org

National Energy Education Development Project
www.need.org

National Energy Foundation
www.nef1.org

National Renewable Energy Laboratory
(see above)

North Carolina Solar Center
www.ncsc.ncsu.edu

Northeast Sustainable Energy Association
www.nesea.org

Solar Now Project
www.solarnow.org

Southface Energy Institute
www.southface.org

U.S. Energy Information Administration
www.eia.doe.gov

Conservation and Efficiency Resources

Building America Program, U.S. Department of Energy
www.eere.energy.gov/buildings/building_america

Database of State Incentives for Renewables and Efficiency
www.dsireusa.org

Energy Star (see above)

Residential Energy Services Network
www.natresnet.org

Tax Incentives Assistance Project
www.energytaxincentives.org

Passive Heating and Cooling Resources

Energy Efficiency & Renewable Energy Clearinghouse
www.eren.doe.gov/consumerinfo
Home Energy Saver
hes.lbl.gov/

National Association of Home Builders— Home Innovation Research Labs
www.homeinnovation.com

National Renewable Energy Laboratory
(see above)

National Solar Thermal Test Facility, Sandia National Laboratories
energy.sandia.gov/?page_id=1267

Southface Energy Institute (see above)

Sustainable Buildings Industries Council
(see above)

Solar Domestic Hot Water Resources

Office of Energy Efficiency and Renewable Energy, U.S. Department of Energy
www.eere.energy.gov/consumer/your_home/water_heating/index.cfm/mytopic=12760

Solar Space Heating Resources

American Society of Heating, Refrigeration, and Air Conditioning Engineers (see above)

American Solar Energy Society (see above)

Hydronic Radiant Heating Association (see above)

National Renewable Energy Laboratory (see above)

Solar Energy Industries Association
(see above)

Solar Electricity Resources

American Solar Energy Society (see above)

Energy Efficiency & Renewable Energy Clearinghouse (see above)

National Association of Home Builders— Home Innovation Research Labs
(see above)

National Renewable Energy Laboratory
(see above)

Northeast Sustainable Energy Association
(see above)

Financing, Incentive, and Rebate Resources

Clean Energy
www.epa.gov/cleanenergy

Database of State Incentives for Renewable Energy (see above)

Interstate Renewable Energy Council
www.irecusa.org

Renewable Energy System Design and Installation Resources

North American Board of Certified Energy Practitioners
www.nabcep.org

The Source for Renewable Energy
www.energy.sourceguides.com/index.shtml

Online Directories of Renewable Energy Installers
www.gosolar.com
www.homepower.com/resources/directory.cfm
www.renewableenergyaccess.com/rea/market/business/home
www.seia.org/about/statechapters.asp

Other Helpful Web Sites

Million Solar Roofs Initiative
www.millionsolarroofs.com

National Center for Photovoltaics
www.nrel.gov/ncpv

Renewable Energy Access
www.renewableenergyaccess.com/rea/home

Renewable Resource Data Center
www.nrel.gov/rredc

Solar Energy Technologies Program
www.eere.energy.gov/solar

Recommended Reading

Baker-Laporte, Paula. *Prescriptions for a Healthy House: A Practical Guide for Architects, Builders and Homeowners*. Gabriola Island, B.C., Can.: New Society Publishers, 2008.

Benson, Tedd. Foreword by Norm Abram. *Timberframe: The Art and Craft of the Post-and-Beam Home*. Newtown, Conn.: Taunton Press, 2001.

Bonin, Jeremy. *Timber Frames: Designing Your Custom Home*. Beachburg, Ont., Can.: Heloconia Press, 2007.

Bonta, Dave, and Stephen Snyder. *New Green Homes Solutions: Renewable Household Energy and Sustainable Living*. Layton, Utah: Gibbs Smith, 2008.

———. *The New Solar Home*. Layton, Utah: Gibbs Smith, 2009.

Farr, Douglas. *Sustainable Urbanism: Urban Design with Nature*. Hoboken, N.J.: John Wiley and Sons, 2008.

Freed, Eric Corey. *Green Building and Remodeling for Dummies*. Hoboken, N.J.: Wiley Publishing, 2008.

Freed, Eric Corey, and Kevin Daum. *GreenSense for the Home: Rating the Real Payoff from Fifty Green Home Projects*. Newtown, Conn.: Taunton Press, 2010.

Green Building Design and Construction. Washington, D.C.: U.S. Green Building Council, 2009.

Green Building Guidelines: Meeting the Demand for Low-Energy, Resource-Efficient Homes. Washington, D.C.: Sustainable Buildings Industry Council, 2007.

Hix, John. *The Glasshouse*. New York: Phaidon, 2005.

Hren, Stephen and Rebekah. *The Carbon-Free Home: Thirty-Six Remodeling Projects to Help Kick the Fossil-Fuel Habit*. White River Junction, Vt.: Chelsea Green Publishing, 2008.

Johnston, David, and Scott Gibson. *Green from the Ground Up: Sustainable, Healthy, and Energy-Efficient Home Construction*. Newtown, Conn.: Taunton Press, 2008.

———. *Toward a Zero Energy Home: A Complete Guide to Energy Self-Sufficiency at Home*. Newtown, Conn.: Taunton Press, 2010.

Kaufmann, Michelle, and Cathy Remick. *PreFab Green*. Layton, Utah: Gibbs Smith, 2009.

Kibert, Charles J. *Sustainable Construction: Green Building Design and Delivery*. Hoboken, N.J.: John Wiley and Sons, 2013.

Knowles, Ralph L. *Ritual House: Drawing on Nature's Rhythms for Architecture and Urban Design*. Washington, D.C.: Island Press, 2006.

Koones, Sheri. *Prefabulous + Almost Off the Grid: Your Path to Building an Energy-Independent Home*. New York: Abrams, 2012.

Kruger, Abe, and Carl Seville. *Green Building: Principles and Practices in Residential Construction*. Clifton Park, N.Y.: Delmar, 2013.

Lubeck, Aaron. *Green Restorations: Sustainable Building and Historic Homes*. Gabriola Island, B.C., Can.: New Society Publishers, 2010.

McDonough, William, and Michael Braungart. *Cradle to Cradle: Remaking the Way We Make Things*. New York: North Point Press, 2002.

Meisel, Ari. *LEED Materials: A Resource Guide to Green Building*. New York: Princeton Architectural Press, 2010.

Racusin, Jacob Deva, and Ace McArleton. *The Natural Building Companion: A Comprehensive Guide to Integrative Design and Construction*. White River Junction, Vt.: Chelsea Green Publishing, 2012.

Ramlow, Bob, and Benjamin Nusz. *Solar Water Heating: A Comprehensive Guide to Solar Water and Space Heating Systems*. Gabriola Island, B.C., Can.: New Society Publishers, 2010.

Roberts, Jennifer. *Redux: Designs that Reuse, Recycle, and Reveal*. Layton, Utah: Gibbs Smith, 2005.

7group and Bill Reed. *The Integrative Design Guide to Green Building: Redefining the Practice of Sustainability*. Hoboken, N.J.: John Wiley and Sons, 2009.

Snell, Clarke, and Tim Callahan. *Building Green: A Complete How-To Guide to Alternative Building Methods*. Asheville, N.C.: Lark Books, 2009.

Spiegel, Ross, and Dru Meadows. *Green Building Materials: A Guide to Product Selection and Specification*. Hoboken, N.J.: John Wiley and Sons, 2012.

Stang, Alanna, and Christopher Hawthorne. *The Green House: New Directions in Sustainable Architecture*. New York: Princeton Architectural Press, 2005.

Susanka, Sarah, with Kira Obolensky. *The Not So Big House: A Blueprint for the Way We Really Live*. Newtown, Conn.: Taunton Press, 2008.

Torres, Martha. *Affordable Home Design: Innovations and Renovations*. New York: Harper Design, 2005.

Wilson, Alex, and Mark Piepkorn, eds. *Green Building Products: The GreenSpec Guide to Residential Building Materials*. Brattleboro, Vt.: BuildingGreen, 2008.

Photography Credits

Numbers refer to page numbers.

Antonio Cuellar
www.antoniocuellarphotography.com
184, 185, 186, 189, 190–91

Matt Dula
www.mdulaphoto.com
178–79, 180–81

Doug Edmunds
www.edmundsstudios.com
99, 100, 101, 102, 103, 104–5

Great Island Photography
www.greatislandphotography.com
14, 15, 16, 17, 18, 19

John Hix Studios
johnhixarchitect.com
1, 9, 82, 83, 84–85, 86, 87, 88–89, 90, 91

Paul Hultberg
38, 39, 40–41, 42–43, 44–45, 46, 47, 48–49

Karant + Associates
www.karant.com
176, 177, 182–83

Rob Karosis
www.robkarosis.com
2–3, 30, 31, 32–33, 35, 36–37

David A. Lee
www.DavidALeePhotography.com
65, 66, 67

Nic Lehoux
www.niclehoux.com
192, 193, 194–95, 196, 197, 198–99,
200–201, 202, 203

John Edward Linden
www.johnlindenphotographs.com
20, 21, 22, 23, 24, 25, 26, 27, 28, 29

John J. Macaulay
106, 107, 108–9, 110, 111, 112–13

Charles Mayer
www.cmayerphoto.com
171, 172, 173, 174–75

Peter Murdock
www.petermurdock.com
92, 93, 94, 95, 96, 97

Tom Olcott
www.tgolcott.com
68, 69, 70, 71, 72, 73

Frank Ooms
www.frankooms.com
6, 115, 116, 117, 118, 119

J. D. Peterson
www.jdpetersonphotography.com
150, 151, 153, 154, 155, 156, 157, 158–59, 160,
161, 162–63

Augusta Quirk
www.laarchitecturalphotographer.com
51, 52–53, 54, 55, 56, 57, 59

Robert Reck Photography
www.robertreck.com
7, 120, 121, 122–23, 124, 125

Barry Rustin Photography
www.barryrustinphotography.com
74, 75, 76, 77, 78, 79, 80–81

Mark Singer Photography
www.marksinger.com
61, 62, 63, 64

Romina Tonucci
www.buildordie.com/people/romina-tonucci
187, 188

E. Spencer Toy
www.sunset.com
10, 11, 12, 13

David Stark Wilson
www.dswdesign.com
4, 204, 205, 206, 207, 208, 209, 210, 211, 212, 213,
214, 215, 216, 217, 218, 219